**Quality Games
for Trainers**

Quality Games for Trainers

101 Playful Lessons in Quality and Continuous Improvement

Marlene Caroselli

McGraw-Hill

New York   San Francisco   Washington, D.C.   Auckland   Bogotá
Caracas   Lisbon   London   Madrid   Mexico City   Milan
Montreal   New Delhi   San Juan   Singapore
Sydney   Tokyo   Toronto

Library of Congress Cataloging-in-Publication Data

Caroselli, Marlene.
    Quality games for trainers : 101 playful lessons in quality and
continuous improvement / Marlene Caroselli.
        p.   cm.
    Includes index.
    ISBN 0-07-011503-6 (pb). — ISBN 0-07-011502-8 (looseleaf)
    1. Total quality management—Study and teaching—Handbooks,
manuals, etc.   2. Management games—Handbooks, manuals, etc.
    3. Employees—Training of—Handbooks, manuals, etc.   I. Title.
HD62.15.C358   1995
658.4'013—dc20   95-40601
                                                                CIP

1 2 3 4 5 6 7 8 9 0 EDW / EDW 9 0 0 9 8 7 6 5 (Looseleaf)
1 2 3 4 5 6 7 8 9 0 EDW / EDW 9 0 0 9 8 7 6 5 (Paperback)

PN 0-07-011647-4 PART OF ISBN 0-07-011502-8 (Looseleaf)
ISBN 0-07-011503-6 [Paperback]

The sponsoring editor for this book was Richard Narramore, the editing supervisor was Fred Dahl, and the production supervisor was Donald Schmidt. It was set in Futura Light by Inkwell Publishing Services.

Printed and bound by Edwards Brothers, Inc.

CONTENTS

KEY QUALITY TRAINING CONCEPTS

PREFACE

Quality Games for Trainers is the output of much thinking, much reading, much writing, much discussing, and much teaching about the principles involved in the Total Quality Management (TQM) movement. This movement, which has been likened to a religion, has converts throughout the world—all determined to reduce waste and inefficiency, all committed to optimizing employees' contributions.

If you conduct training in organizations—as either an internal or external consultant—you will find these games a natural supplement to, and a reinforcer of, the knowledge you are presenting in your training programs *and* the skills you are attempting to develop. You may also wish to use the games to start weekly staff meetings, to publish in the company newsletter, or to share with others who are, formally or informally, spreading the word about Quality.

Even if you are not currently working in a Quality environment, you will find many of these games convertible to any situation in which people seek to effect positive organizational change.

BOOK FORMAT

The book is divided into twelve sections, each paralleling an aspect of Total Quality. Within each section are subcategories reflecting the major concepts of the section heading. These concepts are delineated in an Overview, which can be duplicated and distributed to participants as:

✓ *Take-home reading assignments:* Participants can tell what they could do as a result of what they read.

✓ *Small-group projects:* Brief responses to the Overview can be presented to the whole class.

✓ *Special assignments for individuals who finish a given assignment ahead of others.*

✓ *Breakout activities for participants who have had extensive training in aspect of Quality:* Such individuals can prepare brief lessons, incorporating the Overview points with other training they have received.

✓ *Overview reading assignments:* The entire class can be asked to read the Overview. Then working in small groups, they can formulate three questions about it. (Groups that have prior knowledge of TQM can be asked to list three additional bits of information.)

These field-tested games should be viewed as supplements to your Quality training, not as substitutes for it. (If you do not have a Quality training program, the games can be used in informal training—at the beginning of staff meetings, for example. They can be used as an ongoing series in the company newsletter or used by managers when they address large groups of employees. The quotes alone serve as valuable sources of inspiration. Other informal training uses include bulletin board "teasers" or handouts to celebrate National Quality month.)

The lessons can be incorporated into other training sessions. To illustrate, if you are teaching a course on customer satisfaction, use Section 5 in its entirety. A course on team building can be enhanced with exercises from Section 6 ("Roles Quality Advocates Play") or Section 8 ("Team Meetings"). For various management/supervision/employee issues, the lessons provide supplements that are both fun and fundamental. The lessons in Section 9, "Problem-Solving Tools," for example, offer solid information about cognitive processes, juxtaposed with activities that truly get the cerebral juices flowing.

NATURE OF THE ACTIVITIES

The eight or nine games in each section are designed to help participants understand and appreciate particular nuggets of Quality knowledge.

By *games* we mean short, interactive, fast-paced activities with few restrictions on their sequence or use. As opposed to lessons that teach a sophisticated skill or concept—how to statistically control processes, for example—the activities here are more like icebreakers, warm-ups, brainteasers, fillers, quizzes, self-assessments, etc. (They are sometimes referred to as "sponge" activities, because they can be expanded or contracted as needed, and they are light and easy to manipulate.) Usually some kind of competition is involved, along with a lighthearted focus.

You can pick and choose among the games. There is no need to follow the order within the section or even the order among the sections. Unlike the lesson plans within a module, which are tightly sequential and interdependent, these games can be selected at will and used:

✓ At the beginning of a class

✓ Before and after a break

✓ To introduce a concept

✓ At the end of a difficult or tedious task

✓ To reinforce concepts taught in other lessons

✓ As a change of pace

✓ When only a few minutes remain in an instructional block

✓ When one team is finished working and the others are not. Rather than have the faster team drift out for a break or stay in the room, talking about non-Quality issues, you can engage them in a game until the other teams are through.

OBJECTIVE

Each game begins with a statement of the objective. Although we call these activities "games," they are not "all fun and games." They are enjoyable work— not mindless busywork. Each is directly related to a Quality principle, and each contains the elements found in any good lesson plan, beginning with the objective. The objective also offers a specific tie-in to an aspect of Quality (written in boldface). The tie-in encourages participants to examine one aspect of Total Quality Management. (Key concepts from the objectives appear alphabetically in the Key Quality Training Concepts listed at the front of the book.)

TIME

The length of time ranges from 5 minutes to an hour.

MATERIALS

For the most part, few materials are required. The games are designed with user-friendliness in mind. Complex rules and excessive preparation can destroy the spontaneity and lightheartedness of the games. It is assumed that participants have their own paper and pencils.

MINILECTURE

The minilectures are written in italics to indicate that the trainer will use these words to connect the game with a Quality concept. The minilecture next gives directions for playing the game.

The quotation that appears at the beginning of each lesson can easily be woven into the minilecture, or it can be copied onto a transparency or chart paper and displayed in the classroom. Twenty-five of the quotations appear in the Appendix, along with suggestions for their use.

STEPS TO FOLLOW

Since humans are easily bored, and participants in training programs are more human than most, the procedure sections of each game offer a variety of methods to pique and maintain interest. Some of the activities require team participation; others are solo ventures. Some are highly competitive, while others require contemplation. Some are gamelike, and others depend on creative input. But regardless of the method or the materials, the games all reflect a principle on which the Quality movement is founded.

DISCUSSION QUESTIONS

To further the learning derived from the games, a set of questions is included in each lesson plan. The discussion evoked by the questions encourages the application of Quality ideas to the participants' workplaces.

GAME STRETCHER

Many games offer variations on the basic theme of the game. If time permits, the trainer can explore these suggestions for extending the activity to reinforce the purpose and/or playfulness of the game.

Whenever you can, extend the learning that these games and your own lectures develop. Be creative in your application of the Quality principles emphasized here. Think of ways you can bring others into the instructional loop normally reserved for class attendees. The more global our thoughts about Quality, the more effectively we can work locally.

It is hoped that the pleasure of writing these games will parallel the pleasure experienced by those playing them. Enjoy.

Marlene Caroselli

SECTION 1
THE QUALITY MOVEMENT

Some believe the Quality movement began in America back in 1924 when Dr. Walter Shewhart devised the first control chart for statistically determining the degree of variation in manufacturing processes.

For most people, though, the movement is thought of in more recent terms—the visits of Dr. W. Edwards Deming and Dr. Joseph M. Juran to Japan following World War II.

The principles they taught the Japanese formed the foundation of the Quality philosophy, the texture of which has been enriched by subsequent contributions of other Quality experts such as Philip Crosby, Armand Feigenbaum, Genichi Taguchi, and Kaoru Ishikawa. This section presents the basic concepts of that philosophy and outlines the contributions made by its leading authorities.

OVERVIEW: BASIC PHILOSOPHY

View the body of knowledge we call "Quality" as having both a "hard" side and a "soft" side.

The hard side of quality is the data-driven side, which includes the statistical control of processes as espoused by Dr. Deming, the determination of root cause as encouraged by Philip Crosby, the emphasis placed by Dr. Juran on process capability, and the robust engineering associated with Dr. Taguchi.

On the soft side, we focus on the human relations aspects of Quality—teamwork, empowerment, customer satisfaction, leadership, etc. A book of Quality games is not intended to teach statistical principles. For this reason, the activities here concentrate more on the soft side of Quality than on the hard side.

Those basic principles follow. A game illustrating each of them is found on the following pages.

1. *Quality can be defined as meeting customer needs and reasonable expectations.* Of course, sometimes customer expectations seem unreasonable and customers do not even know what they expect. The flip side of the customer coin contains knowledge that customers possess and that providers need to obtain. That is why Total Quality is often considered a two way education process.

2. *A belief in continuous improvement lies at the heart of the Quality philosophy.* Steeped in a tradition of relentlessly pursuing perfection, the Quality philosophy encourages us to take long hard looks at the way we conduct business—on both the individual and the institutional levels. There is always room for improvement and Quality advocates know the search for excellence is never-ending.

3. *Teams tackle the improvement projects with periodic input from the organization's Quality Council.* Typically composed of members of senior management, the Council ascertains what needs to be done, in terms of improving the organization's competitive position, and who needs to do it. The Council also secures necessary resources and grants approval at various stages of the team's progress.

4. *Because the people closest to the process usually know it best, they should be empowered to make decisions regarding the process.* While such thinking digresses from the Frederick Taylor model of supervisor as omniscient controller, it nonetheless provides a fitting management style for these chaotic times. Trusting employees—as individuals and as team members—to

make decisions about processes that they control causes new links to be forged in chain of quality.

5. *The decisions are based on data.* For managers and team members alike, data-based decision making helps organizations avoid mistakes that ensue when organizations rush to solve problems mistakenly perceived as critical *and* the mistakes that ensue when they don't rush to solve problems that indeed are critical. Data gathering also prevents people from being blamed for problems that are the result of the system's failure.

6. *Benchmarking permits organizations to engage in continuous improvement by learning about the Quality practices in other organizations.* This practice of learning about "best practices" from other companies and then applying them to our own processes is integral to Quality operations. Innovation is encouraged through such comparisons, as is the continuous improvement of processes.

1

MEETING CUSTOMER NEEDS

OBJECTIVES
To develop understanding of the direct role of the customer in achieving **customer satisfaction** and the indirect role in making **continuous improvement** to a process or product

To develop participants' **communication skills**

TIME
Approximately 15 minutes

MATERIALS
Handout 1-1: Communicating as a Customer

MINILECTURE
Marshall Field was a famed department store owner who once observed:

> *Those who enter to buy, support me. Those who come to flatter, please me. Those who complain, teach me how I may please others so that more will come. Only those hurt me who are displeased but do not complain. They refuse me permission to correct my errors and thus improve my service.*

He felt he could be hurt by the dissatisfied customer who did not complain. Not being aware of the problem, Field was unable to correct it. And, if he did not correct it, he was not improving his business. Why do customers not complain? [Allow a few seconds for responses.] One of the reasons is that people are too busy. Another is that they feel no one would listen to the complaint anyway. Another reason is that people feel uncomfortable expressing their dissatisfaction.

Today you will have an opportunity to take a difficult situation and find a way for the customer to express his or her concern without resorting to insult at one extreme or ineffectual niceties at the other. The scenarios are based on real-life situations. The best way to issue a complaint—knowing the best organizations actively seek to hear those complaints—is to avoid sarcasm, anger, profanity, and belittling remarks. State the facts clearly and explain what you would like to have done.

STEPS TO FOLLOW
1. Distribute the worksheet and have participants work in groups of three or four to specify how best to complain.
2. After about 10 minutes, call on each group to share with the whole class one of the responses they thought was especially good.

DISCUSSION QUESTIONS

✓ When was the last time you complained in your role as customer?

✓ How diplomatic were you?

✓ How successful were you?

✓ How does your organization solicit input from customers? How does your department do that? How do you, as an individual?

GAME STRETCHER

(10-20 minutes) Make a list of do's/don'ts for the person making the complaint. To continue the activity for another 10 minutes, have teams work on do's/don'ts for the person handling the complaint.

COMMUNICATING AS A CUSTOMER

Read the following brief scenarios. Then select one and write a 10- to 20-line script depicting an ideal communication between the dissatisfied customer and the individual (representative of the organization) that supplied a product or service.

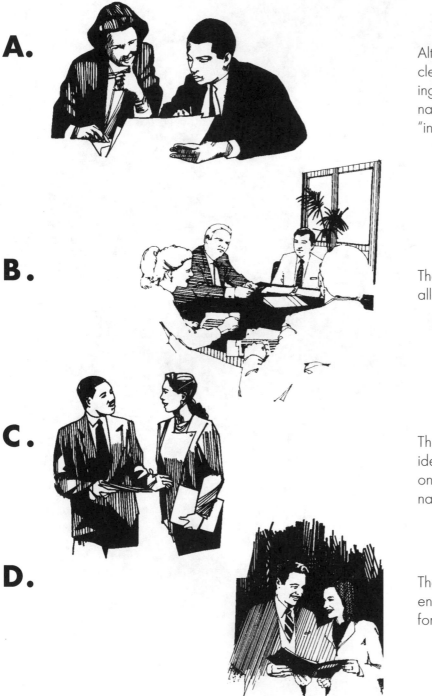

A. Although the supervisor failed to give clear initial directions, he is now criticizing the subordinate's work. (Subordinates, in such a position, are actually "internal customers.")

B. The team member feels the team leader allows too much digression from topic.

C. The sales representative is sharing ideas with the marketing person, based on complaints she has had from external customers.

D. The accounting clerk is explaining to the engineer the sections of the requisition form that he often overlooks.

2

CONTINUOUS IMPROVEMENT

OBJECTIVE   To trace a series of improvements in a given product as an illustration of the concept of **continuous improvement**

TIME   Approximately 15 minutes

MATERIALS   Handout 2-1: In Search of (Continuous) Excellence

MINILECTURE   *When organizations have the habit of excellence, they work to bring improvement on a daily basis to the products/services they provide. As Aristotle remarked, the habit causes excellence in daily acts: "We are what we repeatedly do. Excellence, then, is not an act, but a habit." We'll examine now some of the improvements everyday products have undergone and then think about improvements in our own work.*

STEPS TO FOLLOW   **1.** Distribute the worksheet and have participants work in groups of three or four to discuss improvements that have been made in the products listed.

2. After about 10 minutes, call on several groups to share with the whole class the history of improvement for one of the products cited.

DISCUSSION QUESTIONS   ✓ What changes has your organization's product or service undergone in the last 10 years?

✓ What has caused the changes? (Consider customer input, too.)

✓ What improvements have you made to the work you do?

GAME STRETCHER   (10 minutes) Ask how many people consider themselves creative. Select four or five of those individuals to lead teams that will discuss the improvements that may be made to one or more of the products/services (on the worksheet) in the future. They will ask, "What will this look like/be like ten years from now? Twenty years? Fifty years? [*Note:* If no one identified him-/herself as creative, simply appoint leaders for groups of eight or nine.]

IN SEARCH OF (CONTINUOUS) EXCELLENCE

As you think about and discuss one of the familiar products/services listed below, trace the improvements that have been made over the years to this product or service. If time permits, consider some of the additional products/services at the bottom of the worksheet.

A.

B.

C.

D.

E. Surgery	**F.** Education	**G.** Grocery markets
H. Clothing	**I.** Airplanes	**J.** Mail delivery

3

TEAM PROJECTS

OBJECTIVE   To demonstrate **teamwork** required in assessing worth of possible **projects to continuously improve work processes and work environment**

TIME   Approximately 20 minutes

MATERIALS   Chart paper and marking pens; Transparencies 3-1a: Projects Defined and 3-1b: Yes Assessment

MINILECTURE   *Quality will be accomplished project by project and in no other way." Who could dispute the truth of Dr. Juran's assertion? Yet, teams sometimes neglect—in their enthusiasm to undertake quality improvement projects—to assess the project carefully before they begin. As a result, some teams wind up engaged in what is disdainfully called "recreational TQM." After your team has brainstormed some possible projects, it will subject those project ideas to the Yes Assessment.*

STEPS TO FOLLOW

1. Have teams of five or six brainstorm 10 possible projects that teams in their organizations could work on. They will place a star beside the one they feel would be most beneficial to explore.

2. Next, show the Projects Defined transparency and ask if their starred project falls within the definition given.

3. Finally, ask them to assess their starred project via the Yes Assessment questions on the transparency. Ideally, they will have six yesses.

DISCUSSION QUESTIONS

✓ Do your teams undertake a similar scrutiny of possible projects?

✓ Who in your organization grants approval for teams to proceed?

✓ What additional questions could be asked to ensure the work we do is truly adding value for the customer?

PROJECTS DEFINED

Quality improvement teams work on projects. Those projects may be defined in one of three ways:

1. A process that needs to be improved
   Example: Approval process takes too long.

2. A problem that needs to be solved
   Example: Morale is low.

3. A project that would improve the quality of work life or, indirectly, the quality of the product or service provided.
   Example: Sponsoring an industrywide consortium

YES ASSESSMENT

1. Does this project parallel the organizational mission?

2. Is senior management likely to approve it?

3. Does it offer substantial benefits to the organization?

4. Would customers be likely to approve it?

5. Will the projected costs be considered acceptable?

6. Can our team complete this project in a reasonable period of time?

4

THE PROCESS OWNER AS DECISION MAKER

OBJECTIVES

To develop pride in participants' knowledge of their jobs

To increase the possibility they will seek **greater empowerment**

To illustrate the concept of **decision making at the lowest possible level**

TIME

Approximately 20 minutes

MATERIALS

Transparency 4-1: Pride of Ownership

MINILECTURE

We sometimes forget how very knowledgeable we are about the work we do. In fact, many of us know our jobs better than our bosses know our jobs. An anonymous but widely quoted phrase reflects this fact: "Nobody knows your job like you know your job." Your boss, after all, has a different job to do. Given the fact that the people closest to the process usually know the process best, answer the questions I am about to share with you. Then have your partner complete the same statements. The two of you will then share your answers.

STEPS TO FOLLOW

1. Ask participants to work in pairs. Ask the first question on the transparency and allow sufficient time for each pair-member to complete it. Continue with the remaining questions.

2. Now that they have had a chance to think about their knowledge of and commitment to their jobs, ask how many would be willing to ask their bosses for more decision-making opportunities.

DISCUSSION QUESTIONS

✓ What suggestions do you have for someone who would like to increase the degree of empowerment he or she currently has?

✓ What holds bosses back from granting greater decision-making authority to subordinates?

✓ What holds employees back from asking for this authority?

PRIDE OF OWNERSHIP

1. How long have you been doing this particular job? What have you learned about it?

2. To what extent do you make decisions concerning it?

3. What was the last thing you did to improve the output of one process related to the job?

4. What other ideas do you have for improving processes?

5. Of what are you most proud (in reference to your job)?

6. What would someone who replaced you need to know about it?

5

DATA-DRIVEN DECISIONS

OBJECTIVE   To encourage the **use of appropriate data in decision making**

TIME   Approximately 20 minutes

MATERIALS   Handout 5-1: Enough Data?

MINILECTURE   *If there are going to be any visceral decisions around here, I'd like to use my own viscera." So sayeth IBM's founder, Thomas J. Watson, Jr. in an effort to discourage intuitive decision making. Too much data can slow down decision making; not enough data may lead to regretably hasty decisions. The hard part of decision making is knowing when and if enough is enough. Today, I will share five problems with you. Working in small groups, you will decide if you have enough information to solve the problem. If so, you will then proceed to do exactly that.*

STEPS TO FOLLOW

1. Distribute the worksheet and have participants work in groups of four or five to solve the problems.

2. Afterwards, share the answers, all of which were "enough" for the following reasons:

    a. By stripping away negative connations of certain words and focusing on neutral or literal connotations, you soon realize this is a baseball game in action.

    b. The team leader has red hair, the facilitator black hair. There are four possible answers here: true-true; true-false; false-true, and false-false. The first answer (true-true) is not correct, because we know that at least one statement is false. It can't be the second answer or the third either because—in both scenarios—if one lied, then the other could not have been telling the truth. Thus, the only possible answer is the last one: They both lied.

    c. Obvious but true: a hole.

    d. The probability is zero. If nine teams have their own proposals, then the tenth must too.

    e. The answer is "even." Think about it this way: If you asked everyone in the organization how many hands he or she has shaken, the total would have to be even. This is because each handshake would have been counted twice—one time each by the two individuals engaged in the handshaking. (A cluster of numbers with an even sum cannot have an odd number of odd numbers.)

14

DISCUSSION QUESTIONS

✓ If yours was a team that had all the answers correct, what factors contributed to your success?

✓ If your team missed some answers, what factors led you in the wrong direction?

✓ Think about the last poor decision you made. Did you have too much or not enough data as you made it?

✓ Can you recall an instance in which an incorrect interpretation of a given word caused a problem or prevented one from being solved?

GAME STRETCHER

(10 minutes) Ask participants if they have similar problems that are favorites of theirs. Call on a few participants to come forward and share them.

ENOUGH DATA?

As you consider the following problems, decide if you have enough data to solve the problem. If so, proceed to solve it. If you feel there is insufficient information, check the box marked insufficient and move on to the next problem. At least one of these problems can be solved with the data given.

a. Six members of a quality improvement team had plans for afterwork socializing. As they arrived at their destination, they spotted a man in uniform running home. The man suddenly noticed another man, wearing a mask and holding a dreaded object. The first man turned around and ran back to the place he had come from. Can you tell where the team members are?

☐ Insufficient information to solve the problem
☐ Sufficient information.　Answer: _____

_____

b. A team leader and a facilitator are discussing an upcoming meeting. "I am the team leader," says the one with black hair. "And I am the facilitator," says the one with red hair. If at least one of them is not telling the truth, can you tell who is lying?

☐ Insufficient information to solve the problem
☐ Sufficient information.　Answer: _____

_____

c. Six members of a quality improvement team are chatting before their meeting begins. One of them holds up his half-filled coffee cup and says, "What can I put in here that is weightless, can be seen by all of you, and will make this half-filled coffee cup weigh less than it does right now?" Can this problem, as stated, be solved?

☐ Insufficient information to solve the problem
☐ Sufficient information.　Answer: _____

_____

d. Ten quality improvement teams had prepared proposals to share with the organization's Quality Council. A temporary secretary, unfortunately, removed all the cover pages before returning the proposals to the teams. What is the probability that only nine of the ten teams had their own proposals returned to them?

☐ Insufficient information to solve the problem
☐ Sufficient information.　Answer: _____

_____

e. Think about the total number of people in your organization who may have shaken hands with an odd number of people. Is the *total number* (of people in your organization who have shaken hands with an odd number of people) odd or even?

☐ Insufficient information to solve the problem
☐ Sufficient information.　Answer: _____

_____

OVERVIEW: LEADING PROPONENTS

Dr. W. Edwards Deming died in 1993, at the age of 93. For decades, his voice—which continues to be heard—codified the principles and practices that now constitute Total Quality Management. (Although he objected to the use of the term, we continue to use it for easy reference to a philosophy whose initials most businesspeople are familiar with.) Deming's Fourteen Points comprise the essence of his Quality views. Dr. Deming called for well defined systems, asserting that the more complex the system, the more critical the need for good communication among the system parts.

14 POINTS OF MANAGEMENT

1. Create constancy of purpose toward improvement of product and service.
2. Adopt the new philosophy. We can no longer live with commonly accepted levels of delays, mistakes, defective materials, and defective workmanship.
3. Cease dependence on mass inspection. Require, instead, statistical evidence that quality is built-in.
4. End the practice of awarding business on the basis of price tag.
5. Find problems. It is management's job to work continually on the system.
6. Institute modern methods of training on the job.
7. Institute modern methods of supervision of production workers. The responsibility of supervisors must be changed from numbers to quality.
8. Drive out fear so that everyone may work effectively for the company.
9. Break down barriers between departments.
10. Eliminate numerical goals, posters, and slogans for the workforce that ask for new levels of productivity without providing methods.
11. Eliminate work standards that prescribe numerical quotas.
12. Remove barriers that stand between hourly workers and their right to pride of workmanship.
13. Institute a vigorous program of education and retraining.
14. Create a structure in top management that supports the preceding 13 points every day.

Dr. Joseph M. Juran, is retired from the Juran Institute, but delivering a series of lectures called "The Last Word." He, too, set forth his Quality credo in a number of steps that clearly and precisely enable organizations to undertake their journeys. Juran is the recipient of Emperor Hirohito's Award for having taught the Japanese quality principles that helped revolutionize their manufacturing processes. Juran insists management take responsibility for raising the corporate levels of quality. This is a responsibility, he maintains, that cannot be delegated.

10 STEPS TO QUALITY IMPLEMENTATION

1. Build awareness of the need and opportunity for improvement.
2. Set goals for improvement.
3. Organize to reach the goals (establish a Quality Council, identify problems, select projects, appoint teams, designate facilitator).
4. Provide training.
5. Carry out projects to solve problems.
6. Report progress.
7. Give recognition.
8. Communicate results.
9. Keep score.
10. Maintain momentum by making annual improvement part of the regular systems and processes of the company.

Philip M. Crosby established Crosby College to train businesspeople about his version of Quality. Famous for coining expressions such as "zero defects" and "do it right the first time," Crosby has synthesized his views on Quality in a 14-point declaration. Strongly humanistic in his views, Crosby tells us that we should "always assume that people are vitally interested in the quality improvement process." He then assures us that people will act to fulfill our conviction. "Assume the best and that is usually what happens," he encourages us.

14 STEPS TO QUALITY IMPROVEMENT

1. Make it clear that management is committed to quality.
2. Form quality improvement teams with representatives from each department.
3. Determine where current and potential quality problems lie.
4. Evaluate the quality awareness and personal concern of all employees.
5. Raise the quality awareness and personal concern of all employees.
6. Take actions to correct problems identified through previous steps.
7. Establish a committee for the zero defects programs.
8. Train supervisors to actively carry out their part of the quality improvement program.
9. Hold a "zero defects day" to let all employees realize that there has been a change.
10. Encourage individuals to establish improvement goals for themselves and their groups.
11. Encourage employees to communicate to management the obstacles they face in attaining their improvement goals.
12. Recognize and appreciate those who participate.
13. Establish Quality Councils to communicate on a regular basis.
14. Do it all over again to emphasize that the quality improvement program never ends.

6

DR. W. EDWARDS DEMING

OBJECTIVE   To develop the ability to give **positive feedback**, thus minimizing the potential loss of ideas (a loss the **Deming philosophy** cautions us to avoid)

TIME   Approximately 15 minutes

MATERIALS   None

MINILECTURE   *How feedback is given to someone who offers an idea either encourages further ideas to be shared or ensures that no other contributions will be made. These other contributions that will never be made represent the losses to which Dr. Deming alludes when he tells us that "the greatest losses are unknown and unknowable."*

The manager who, for example, replies, "That's the dumbest thing I've ever heard," has several messages in the subtext of his or her comment. Such a reply suggests a lack of respect, a lack of receptivity to new ideas, a management style characterized by fear, and a wish to have subordinates view the world the way the manager views the world. Certainly, each of us is allowed to think, "That's the dumbest thing I've ever heard," but we need to express non agreement in a way that does not decimate the individual making a proposal.

You will work with two others now in a role play situation. One of you will propose a bad idea (about training, the work environment, computers, cultural diversity, or anything work-related). The second person will play the part of the boss who will listen to the idea, and then turn it down in such a way that the proposer will feel encouraged to present an even better idea the next time. The third person in your group will be the observer offering feedback on the exchange to both of you.

In the next two sets of role plays, the proposer will become the manager and then the observer so that each person in your group will have an opportunity to play all three roles.

STEPS TO FOLLOW   **1.** Arrange groups of three. [*Note:* If one person is left, you can role play with him or her. If two are left, they can engage in the role play without an observer.]

2. After three rounds of role play, call on each group to share one tip or technique that seemed to be effective.

DISCUSSION QUESTIONS

✓ How does your boss typically receive suggestions?

✓ Do you know any famous business examples of a good idea that was not initially well received, and yet ultimately became successful? (One good example is the founding of the Xerox Corporation.)

GAME STRETCHER

(5 minutes) Compile a master list of tips for giving negative feedback in a positive manner. Keep it posted in the training room and refer to it on future occasions when someone demonstrates a technique that worked especially well in a feedback situation.

7

DR. JOSEPH M. JURAN

OBJECTIVE　　　To identify common components in **Quality philosophies**

TIME　　　Approximately 15 minutes

MATERIALS　　　None

MINILECTURE　　　*There are some differences in the basic philosophies of the Quality movement's top advocates. But—as some have asked—if they are all slaying the same dragon, does it really matter what kind of sword they are using? Your job today is to find what constitutes that metaphorical dragon. What aspects of Quality do all three gurus emphasize?*

STEPS TO FOLLOW

1. Allow five minutes for participants to skim the philosophies of the three gurus in the preceding Overviews. Then have them form small groups of five or six.

2. They are to find at least five common threads in the basic philosophies of Quality's three most famous spokesmen. [*Note:* All three gurus emphasize change for example. Another thread running through all of their philosophies is recognition of workers. Yet another is their support of training.]

DISCUSSION QUESTIONS

✓ Organizations typically have people or departments engaged in "turf wars." Such wars are typically won when all work units come to realize and accept the benefits of working together—of fighting the "same dragons." Dr. Juran himself exhorts us to "eliminate turf wars." What positive and negative aspects of your work environment could serve to unify the workforce, assuming common understandings of those aspects could be attained?

✓ What common understandings bind your organization to similar organizations throughout the nation?

GAME STRETCHER　　　(5–10 minutes) For each of the common "dragon" threads listed, have participants assess on a scale of 1 to 5, how successfully their organizations are dealing with the aspect listed.

8

PHILIP B. CROSBY

OBJECTIVE To identify **value** brought to **work processes**

TIME Approximately 10 minutes

MATERIALS None

MINILECTURE *Quickly—Jot down the greatest contribution you are making or have made to your organization. What are you most proud of? What leadership have you demonstrated? Have you done what Philip Crosby encourages us to do: "Leave footprints instead of just dust"? [Pause.] Now think about what you are likely to be remembered for after you have left or retired. Will you have left footprints or just dust? [Pause.] Are the two things the same? Typically they are not. We as individuals know our value, we know what we bring to the work we do, but for a variety of reasons what we know and what others know are not always the same.*

If you could design your own business card to reflect the best of what you do, what would that card say? Assume the job you do is an enterprise of its own. How would your business card describe the enterprise and the role you play? Be honest but imaginative at the same time. This is no time for modesty.

METHOD Have participants work individually to design their business cards and then to share them with each other.

DISCUSSION QUESTIONS
- ✓ Crosby asserts that it only takes one person to lead the march. What marches have you led (what new practices have you instituted) at work in the last five years?
- ✓ Whom in your organization do you admire for the "footprints" they have left, the marches they have led?
- ✓ How can organizations show they value the contributions employees make and can make?
- ✓ How does the organization benefit—directly and indirectly—when it encourages employees to "leave footprints"?

SECTION 2
CHANGING THE CULTURE

Continuous improvement means continuous change. Many of the changes that occur, to be sure, are incremental, reflecting the essence of the Japanese word *kaizen*. Some aspects of the culture can and should remain constant, of course, Just as some aspects of our individual essence remain constant, no matter what experiences we have.

Yet the culture as a whole should be undergoing a continual stream of calibrations, of adjustment and amendment, of addition and subtraction. In some organizations, radical transformations in the culture are required; in others, a less dramatic redefining is needed.

Questions about what constitutes the culture, what influences it, and how it can be changed, are explored in this section.

OVERVIEW: THE STRUCTURE OF A QUALITY ORGANIZATION

In a Quality organization, the executive level of management is fully committed to Quality principles. Some are committed to broad Total Quality Management principles. They have as their overriding Quality philosophy a combination of the three gurus' ideas melded into a synthesis they call their own. Other organizations are proponents of one specific Quality guru or another.

Ideally, the top level has received training in the Quality philosophy and methodology. It then ensures that everyone else receives the training needed. The training is handled in various ways: by the in-house training department, by bringing external trainers in, by sending employees to training centers, or through a combination of those methods. For example, in some organizations, executives are sent to the Juran Institute or the Crosby College. The senior managers then conduct training themselves to allow the same message to cascade through the various departments.

Beyond commitment and training, another feature of the Quality organization is the establishment of a Quality Council. This body of managers approves the work of the various teams and assists them in obtaining resources. The members of the Council should be high-level managers, for they have sufficient authority to determine if projects are aligned with mission and to allocate resources.

A third distinguishing feature of the Quality organization is teams—some of them cross-functional, others formed from actual work units—that determine how best to improve processes. Training—in team building, in team leadership, and in facilitation—is important if teams are to optimize their efforts.

9

COMMITMENT WITH A CAPITAL C

OBJECTIVE	To promote realization that total commitment can effect **organizational transformations**
TIME	Approximately 10 minutes
MATERIALS	Transparency 9-1: Commitment
MINILECTURE	*If the uppermost levels of corporations tried to turn Dr. Deming over to the vice-presidential levels, Dr. Deming would refuse to work with the corporation. He insisted on commitment from the highest levels on down. Without such commitment, the organization lacks cohesion and the "constancy of purpose" Dr. Deming felt was so important. Individual pockets of commitment to quality are not enough. There must be a seamless fabric that covers the organization.*

Ideally, this kind of "whole hog" commitment, lightheartedly depicted in the following exchange, will permeate the organization:

Chicken: *"I'm committed to giving eggs for breakfast every morning."*

Pig: *"That's not commitment. That's participation. Giving bacon ≡ now that's commitment."*

STEPS TO FOLLOW

1. Ask participants to draw a capital *C*. Allow a moment for them to show one another the types of *C*'s they have drawn.

2. Then display the Commitment transparency and point out the differences between the individual contribution and the consistent, uniform, interlocking *combination* of individual contributions.

DISCUSSION QUESTIONS

✓ To what extent is there participation—as opposed to commitment to Quality in your organization?

✓ On what is commitment based?

✓ If you ran the company, how would you increase commitment?

✓ How can senior management demonstrate its commitment?

GAME STRETCHER

(10 minutes) Assign a different letter of the alphabet to dyads; ask them to create a pattern using only that letter. Discuss how the merged letter takes on a whole new look, as do firms committed to quality.

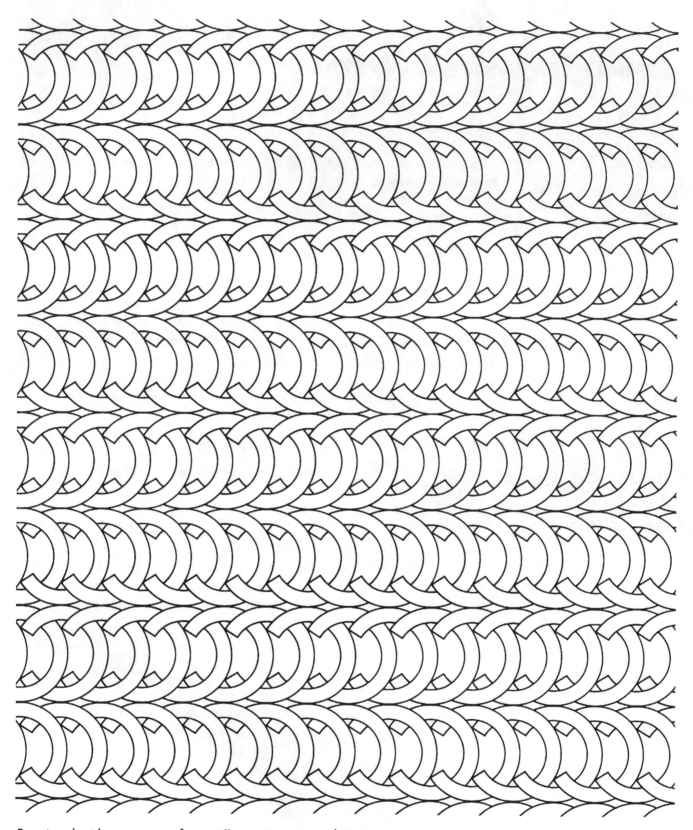

Reprinted with permission from *Allover Patterns with Letter Forms* by Jean Larcher, New York: Dover Publications, Inc.

10

(JOHARI) WINDOW OF OPPORTUNITY

OBJECTIVE To assess the extent of **common knowledge of TQM** and uncommon knowledge as well

TIME Approximately 15 minutes

MATERIALS Flip chart and marking pen

MINILECTURE *More than 30 years ago, Joseph Luft and Harrington Ingram devised a simple set of squares to reveal what we know or don't know about ourselves and what others know or don't know about us. We will use that same window to examine what we know or don't know about Quality. The more we learn, the more rapid the transformation, as noted by Philip Crosby: "The quickest way to turn around is for the management of companies to take charge of the education of their people and help them to learn the necessary things."*

STEPS TO FOLLOW **1.** Ask participants to draw a diagram like the following:

	Things I know about TQM	Things I don't know
Things most others know	1	3
Things most others don't know	2	4

2. They will then fill in the squares (at least three points in each):

1 = Things I know about TQM and most others do too

2 = Things I know but most others do not

3 = Things I don't know about TQM but others seem to know

4 = Things I don't know and others probably don't know either

DISCUSSION QUESTIONS ✓ Which of the four squares should most concern the trainer?

✓ How can we verify the accuracy of these observations?

✓ How can we add to boxes 1 and 2 and subtract from boxes 3 and 4?

GAME STRETCHER (10-40 minutes) Present an opportunity to "do" Quality by having participants teach others the things they listed in boxes 1 and 2.

11

QUALITY COUNSEL

OBJECTIVE

To illustrate how a **Quality Council** functions within the **structure of a Quality organization**

TIME

Approximately 15 minutes

MATERIALS

Transparency 11-1: Quality Council

MINILECTURE

The Quality Council plays an important role in the functioning of a Quality committed organization, as shown in this mission statement from the General Services Administration's Federal Supply Service, Region 3's Quality Council:

> Our purpose is to create an environment in which each employee is able to understand what we do and why, and is encouraged to suggest better ways of doing things. In this light, we promise to provide leadership, remove roadblocks, and demonstrate total commitment to the quality improvement process.

> Typically composed of senior managers, the Council assists teams in the important work teams do. Part of that assistance is guiding the team toward success. Councils evaluate team proposals and recommend that teams proceed, gather more data, or, on occasion, abandon projects that do not appear promising.

STEPS TO FOLLOW

1. Show the Quality Council transparency and have the class decide how the steps should be arranged. (Which step should be first, second, etc.)

2. Before sharing the answers, advise that the sequence you will present is *recommended* (by Anne Marie Acton, Quality Manager for the General Services Administration). It is certainly not the only way a council could orchestrate its work. Step 1 = D; 2 = F; 3 = B; 4 = G; 5 = C; 6 = A; 7 = E; 8 = H.

DISCUSSION QUESTIONS

✓ Does your organization have a Quality Council? Why or why not?

✓ What do you think a Council's mission should state?

✓ What are the functions of the Quality Council?

GAME STRETCHER

(10 minutes) Discuss the answers that differed from the preceding recommended sequence and ask participants to explain their answers.

QUALITY COUNCIL

In what order should a Quality Council undertake these steps?

A. Initiate key supplier/partner relationships.

B. Plan HR policies and goals.

C. Involve all managers.

D. Develop Foundation for Quality Management.

E. Monitor progress and recognize achievement.

F. Plan quality goals and objectives.

G. Charter quality improvement teams.

H. Audit/assess the Quality system.

OBJECTIVE	To develop **teamwork** through awareness of the various **roles team members play**
TIME	Approximately 15 minutes
MATERIALS	None
MINILECTURE	*The team leader cannot be expected to be all things to all people at all times. On occasion, team members need to step in and play a role that is needed to move the team forward. If no one ever served as a "surgeon," for example, teams would be destined to carry around excess organizational "fat." Good teams become great ones by working in concert. As Baltaser Gracian notes, "The path to greatness is always along with others."*

STEPS TO FOLLOW

1. Have small groups recall (or imagine) a meeting situation that needed someone to serve in each of these roles: the devil's advocate, the minister, the coach, the analyzer, and the resuscitator. They should discuss what happened (happens) when someone responded (responds) to the need. They should also discuss what happened (happens) when no one assumes the responsibility of playing the role that is called for in team meetings.

2. Have them join another group to share their answers.

DISCUSSION QUESTIONS

✓ Do team leaders typically explain the need for team members to be multi-faceted?

✓ What are some other roles that could serve a valuable purpose?

✓ How can leaders create an environment in which members feel comfortable playing various roles?

GAME STRETCHER

(10-20 minutes) Conduct role plays on some of the situations described. Appoint one member in each team to play the needed role.

13

ESPRIT DE CORPS

OBJECTIVE
To demonstrate the "rush" people feel at **team meetings** when engaged in projects calling for both **teamwork** and **creativity**

TIME
Approximately 20 minutes

MATERIALS
Flip chart; marking pens; 3×5 cards; Transparency 13-1: Market this!

MINILECTURE
Meetings can be both the worst of times and the best of times for team members. When they fall in the second category, it is usually because the team is united around a common interest, communicating well and advancing creatively toward their mutual goal. To quote Julie Barker: "The key to better communication at meetings, and to more efficiency, may well lie in developing creative thinking."

To demonstrate the heady feeling associated with such progress, you will work in teams on a creative project. Assume you are the marketing department tasked with devising a marketing campaign (complete with product name and advertising slogans). Your company is trying to break into new markets.

STEPS TO FOLLOW

1. Appoint a leader for each team of seven or eight. Assign each team one of the products listed on the transparency.

2. Have team members write one serious idea for the product name and advertising slogan on one side of their 3×5 cards and one wacky idea for each on the other side. Then the leader calls on each person to present his/her ideas. The team will then select their favorite product name and slogan. A spokesperson from each team will share the selection with the whole class.

DISCUSSION QUESTIONS

✓ How did team members feel as the ideas were bouncing around?

✓ How does this feeling differ from the feeling at most meetings?

✓ How did humor affect the members' feelings about each other?

✓ Which ideas might actually work?

MARKET THIS!

1. Quilting bee products for men

2. Women's patronage of barber shops for haircuts

3. Girdles for men

4. Attendance at boxing matches by women

5. Makeup products for men

6. Football equipment for teams composed of women only

OVERVIEW: CREATING A QUALITY ENVIRONMENT

Rhetoric by itself is not enough. If organizational leaders wish to create a Quality environment, Quality must clearly matter. To the fullest extent possible, fear has to be driven from the environment so that employees feel comfortable offering ideas. Those ideas must be listened to and acted on. A Quality environment shows evidence of teamwork and empowerment, proof of continuous learning and continuous improvement, and indications that positive change is being effected.

The primary responsibility for creating that culture lies with top management, who are tasked with making quality a cornerstone of their strategic plans. While the plans for quality cannot be delegated, they can be shared. In this sharing, a new emphasis is brought to the existing culture. When Total Quality initiatives are endorsed by all strata of the workplace culture, then the organization creates a Quality environment, one characterized by employees who assert, "Quality! I take it personally."

For those determined to create such a collective mindset, a good starting point is the definition of Quality. It can mean many things to many people, but typically the term encompasses a focus on customer satisfaction and conformance to increasingly more exact specifications.

Given an agreed-upon understanding of both Quality and Total Quality, training must be extended to the entire workforce so that employees have both the physical and mental tools required to achieve excellence in their performance.

Additionally, the organization must rethink existing structures to better serve customers, employees, and teams. The formation of a Quality Council and even appointments to newly created Quality positions are but a few of the ways the Quality transformation can be undertaken.

14

DEFINING THE ENVIRONMENT

OBJECTIVE	To encourage **clarity in communications** through **common understanding of key terms**
TIME	Approximately 15 minutes
MATERIALS	3∞5 cards
MINILECTURE	*Philip Crosby frequently notes the difficulty of reaching common agreement on what "quality" means. Individually, we have an understanding of what "quality" means to us and yet our separate definitions will probably not be exactly alike. Definitions—once described by an anonymous lexicographer as "statements intended to put words in their place"—are not easily arrived at. Let's take a moment to verify this.*

STEPS TO FOLLOW

1. Ask participants to work in pairs to define the word *quality*. Next, call on several to read their definitions aloud.

2. Form teams of five or six. Have each person jot down five or six words that are integral components of a Quality environment. Then ask one person to begin explaining what he/she wrote. The other members politely interrupt to ask what is meant by certain words. The "definer" must define the terms before proceeding.

3. When the first definer is finished, go on to other members of the group and have them do the same thing, using their respective lists.

DISCUSSION QUESTIONS

✓ Were there any signs of impatience or frustration as the group asked the definer to explain what he or she meant?

✓ How can a team leader avoid this frustration occurring at meetings?

✓ What other key words does management assume everyone knows?

✓ Which key words need definition?

GAME STRETCHER

(5-15 minutes) Have the groups define other words as well. If levity is sought, select words that are related to other activities.

15

THE TRUTH ABOUT LISTENING

OBJECTIVE   To encourage participants to **listen more effectively** by examining facts about listening

TIME   Approximately 20 minutes

MATERIALS   Handout 15-1: The Truth about Listening

MINILECTURE   *How many of you would consider yourselves good listeners? [Pause.] Keep your hand up if you are certain that your spouse (or good friend) would agree with you. How many of you are certain your children would consider you a good listener? Your co-workers? Your boss? Okay. You can put your hands down now. The difference between what we consider to be true about listening and what others consider truth is often very wide. We will explore some of those differences today in a handout designed to develop the "big people" of whom David Schwartz speaks: "Big people monopolize the listening. Small people monopolize the talking."*

STEPS TO FOLLOW

1. Distribute handout. (Share the answers, which are all B, after the next step has been completed.)

2. Once participants have completed the quiz, have them share their answers with a partner. Ask if any pair had exactly the same answers. If so, ask if one member of the pair would volunteer to spend three or four minutes talking about his/her family (or another safe topic). As the person is speaking, periodically interrupt him/her by calling on someone in the audience and asking, "Quick! What was the last point she made?" Typically, participants realize in very little time how much work it takes to listen carefully.

DISCUSSION QUESTIONS

✓ How well do managers in your organization listen to the ideas of their subordinates?

✓ What can an organization do to improve listening across the board?

✓ Why is listening not usually taught in schools?

✓ Can you recall a time when poor listening caused a serious problem?

✓ What traits do effective listeners manifest?

THE TRUTH ABOUT LISTENING

As you read the following statements, circle the response you know is true or believe is true. Each statement has one true response. When you have finished, compare your answers to a partner's.

1. University of Michigan studies show that after two months, people
   a. remember only a tenth of what they heard.
   b. remember a quarter of what they heard.
   c. remember half of what they heard.
   d. remember none of what they heard.

2. They also show that immediately after listening to someone, people
   a. remember everything they heard.
   b. remember most of what they heard.
   c. remember half of what they heard.
   d. remember little of what they heard.

3. Florida State studies show that, within eight hours, people
   a. forget everything they heard.
   b. forget one-third to one-half of what they heard.
   c. forget three-quarters of what they heard.
   d. forget nearly everything they heard.

4. Scientists say our brains can process words at a speed of
   a. 1000 words a minute.
   b. 800 words a minute.
   c. 500 words a minute.
   d. 250 words a minute.

5. University of Michigan studies show that we spend the following percentage of our daily communication time in listening
   a. 85 percent
   b. 45 percent
   c. 25 percent
   d. 15 percent

OVERVIEW: OVERCOMING BARRIERS

Barriers are not always visible. Sometimes the barriers are mindsets, which can be exceedingly difficulty to change. The good news is that we can exert control over more of the barriers than we realize. The bad news is that it won't be easy, but achieving excellence seldom is.

The barriers must first be identified. Guessing or assuming what they are does not lead to identification. Recall the delivery service company that assumed customers were primarily interested in quick pickups and deliveries. They instructed their drivers not to talk to customers but instead to move briskly along their routes. Excessive customer complaints caused them to rethink their assumptions. Similarly, we cannot afford to assume that we understand the barriers preventing employees from doing their best work.

Decision makers attend to identifying barriers and also to determining the goals that the barrier may be preventing us from reaching. Those goals are also assessed to learn which most severely impact profitability, productivity, customer satisfaction, or any other focus the organization values.

Prioritization follows the identification. A governing body decides which barriers can and should be tackled first. Their decisions are then passed along to the teams that will do the work of barrier removal—unless, of course, the barriers are those within management's capacity to remove. (Quality gurus maintain that 85 percent of the causes of poor quality lie in the system, which management controls.) Careful assessment of barriers and the outputs they impact must precede the work of removal.

The barriers are not always physical barriers. We tend to think of outdated equipment, insufficient space, or disorganized files as the barriers that stand between quality and us. But the barriers can exist on many levels—psychological, personal, interpersonal, emotional, etc.

Teams depend on top management's wisdom and sensitivity in ascertaining which obstacles are preventing which values from being accepted. Their wisdom and sensitivity are also needed to help remove today's barriers that are preventing tomorrow's success.

16

REMOVING BARRIERS

OBJECTIVE
To encourage positive attitudes toward **removing barriers** by reminding participants that crises are often **opportunities in disguise**

TIME
Approximately 15 minutes

MATERIALS
Handout 16-1: Heavy Mettle

MINILECTURE
Many times, quality improvement teams become discouraged as they realize the number of barriers that have to be removed before their plans can be realized. Barrier removal, though, can provide excellent opportunities for teams and team members to test their mettle, to discover new paths to success. Two thousand years ago, Horace made reference to the crisis as opportunity: "The very difficulty of a problem evokes abilities or talents which would otherwise, in happy times, never emerge to shine.

STEPS TO FOLLOW
1. Distribute the Heavy Mettle handout and have participants work on it solo for about 10 minutes.

2. Ask if anyone wishes to share his or her thoughts with the class.

DISCUSSION QUESTIONS
✓ How can team leaders use insights such as those evoked by this exercise to keep teams motivated?

✓ Generally speaking, what resources (both inside and outside the organization) are available to teams trying to remove barriers?

✓ Dr. Deming advised removing barriers that stand between the hourly worker and his/her right to pride of workmanship. What are some of those barriers?

GAME STRETCHER
(10-15 minutes) Have participants recall historical events (from the worlds of science, politics, sports, government, art, etc.) that proved ultimately to be positive despite first being viewed as negative.

HEAVY METTLE

Adversity often provides us opportunities to test our mettle, to learn what we are capable of doing. Over-coming the adversity—eliminating the barriers that stand between us and our goals—often effects success that would otherwise not have been known. Consider these situations:

Walt Disney suffered bankruptcy and a nervous breakdown.

Milton Hershey was declared bankrupt. He went on to build an empire based on chocolate.

Edmund McIlhenny's sugar plantation was destroyed in the Civil War. Only wild peppers were left. He developed Tabasco sauce from them. His family is still running the business.

Einstein was called retarded, as was motivational speaker Les Brown.

1. Think of some occasions in your own life about which you now say, "It all turned out for the best." In other words, think of difficult or challenging situations that you worked through and felt good about afterwards.

_____

_____

_____

_____

2. In terms of your career, list the things you are most proud of. What prompted you to do or become the things on that list?

_____

_____

_____

_____

3. Consider the changes your organization has undergone. What crises or temporary barriers to excellence had to be overcome or eliminated?

_____

_____

_____

_____

17

THE FEAR FACTOR

OBJECTIVE   To have participants consider how to **"drive out fear,"** as Dr. Deming encourages us to do

TIME   Approximately 15 minutes

MATERIALS   Handout 17-1: The Fear Factor

MINILECTURE   *"Drive out fear," Dr. Deming tells us, "so that everyone may work effectively for the company." The causes of fear, though, are many and pervasive. When fear runs rampant in the workplace, more than productivity is impaired. Morale, harmony, and the desire to work efficiently slowly erode.*

To eliminate fear, we must first identify it. With this identification, we begin the improvement process. ("Fear is the start of wisdom," Miguel de Unamuno tells us.) Handout 17-1 helps you to identify the symptoms of fear and the circumstances that produce those symptoms.

STEPS TO FOLLOW
1. Distribute the Fear Factor handout and have participants work on it in teams of three. They should feel comfortable sharing *either* personal experiences or hypothetical ones.

2. Call on various groups to share their thoughts.

DISCUSSION QUESTIONS
✓ Think of a wisdom you now possess that began as a fear.

✓ Are there fears that should not be eliminated?

✓ What can be done at the employee level to eliminate fear in the workplace? At the management level?

GAME STRETCHER   (10-20 minutes) Take other words related to emotion (anger, excitement, joy) and list 15 related words for each. Try to select an incident in the workplace that evokes each of the related words.

HANDOUT 17-1

THE FEAR FACTOR

Eliminating fear is obviously easier said than done. But identifying how the fear makes us feel and isolating the circumstances that prompt a certain kind of fear—this is fairly easy to do. From such understanding, actions are born "feelings" that move us away from fear and into wisdom.

Look at the following types of fear. For each, think of a work related circumstance that can evoke this kind of fear. If possible, think of one thing that can be done to improve the circumstance. Use personal experiences *or* hypothetical ones.

1. Panic _____

_____

2. Consternation _____

_____

3. Worry _____

_____

4. Anxiety _____

_____

5. Dread _____

_____

6. Nervousness _____

_____

7. Revulsion _____

_____

8. Dismay_____

_____

9. Awe_____

_____

10. Hesitation _____

_____

SECTION 3

PROCESSES

All work is process. The processes constitute a system. Understanding our individual processes enables us to have a better understanding of the macro-processes and systems on which the organization operates.

Section 3 contains games to reinforce basic Quality principles:

The process begins when a supplier gives us what we need to do our work. We add our value to the process, thus transforming an input to an output. The output is delivered to a customer, who views our output as his/her input. And so another process begins.

OVERVIEW: INPUT

The process begins when we receive an input from someone. The someone who provides us what we need to begin our work is called our *supplier*. Typically, the input is a request to perform some work. The individual who gives us that request is the supplier. Occasionally, the supplier may be oneself. For example, an artist who creates a drawing in the hope of later being able to sell it to an art gallery is prompted by ambition or a creative drive. The input in such a case would be self-motivation.

The supplier may be inside the organization or outside. An inside supplier might be a boss, a co-worker, or even a set of requirements drawn up by other people. An outside supplier might be someone placing an order, which prompts us to begin the first of several processes—the end result of which is the delivery of a product or service to the individual who originally placed the order.

The person who begins the process with an input could, in fact, be the same person who receives the output at the end of the process.

If the input lacks quality, so will the output. It is as simple as that. Process owners cannot create silken outputs if they have been given sows' ears for inputs. Just as computer operators will tell you not to put garbage in because you will surely get garbage out, process owners need to do all they can to ensure that quality is going into the product or service at the very beginning. Process owners have an obligation to speak up if the directions are unclear, if the paperwork is incomplete, or if the widget part is damaged.

One of the most substantial benefits of the drive toward Quality (as in Total Quality Management) and the drive toward quality (as in excellence) is the increased communication between internal customers and suppliers. As we learn more about what others need from us and vice versa, the quality of the ultimate product is bound to improve.

18

THE CUSTOMER-SUPPLIER CHAIN

OBJECTIVES

To realize the **interdependency** of employees: Each is both a customer who receives another employee's **output** (and regards it as an **input**) and a **supplier** who provides his own **output** to another employee (who considers it an **input**)

To develop **effective listening** skills

To provide participants an opportunity to express their thoughts about/**knowledge of TQM**

TIME

Approximately 25 minutes

MATERIALS

None

MINILECTURE

Each of us depends on someone else's output. In that sense, we are a customer to the supplier or the person who provides us with what we need to do our work. We regard that output from another person as our own input, as the thing that begins our work process.

The output of our process is delivered to someone else (our customer) and the cycle begins again. The customer-supplier chain in the workplace requires mutual respect and clear communications to stay unbroken. This interdependency is reflected in Lee Iacocca's feisty observation: "People in engineering and manufacturing almost have to be sleeping together; these guys weren't even flirting."

To illustrate how those workplace links constitute a chain, I'd like to have each of you listen very, very carefully as one person begins a one-minute talk about Quality (referring to TQM) or about quality (referring to excellence in a product or service). The person to the right of the first speaker will take one word spoken by the first speaker, and will use that word as the theme of his or her own one minute talk about Quality.

The next person (to the right of the second speaker) will do the same thing: isolate one word that was spoken and use it as a springboard for his/her own one-minute talk about Quality.

STEPS TO FOLLOW

1. Assemble chairs in a large circle.

2. Start the game by stating something you youÍrself believe about TQM. Or, if the group is extroverted enough, appoint someone else to start.

3. Take notes on a few of the comments being made and use them to supplement the later discussion.

DISCUSSION QUESTIONS

✓ How good were our listening skills?

✓ What did you hear that you agreed with?

✓ What did you hear that is different from what you believe?

✓ What did you hear that you'd like clarification on?

✓ How can we round out the rough edges of thought so that we can all view Quality (or any other topic) from a common perspective?

GAME STRETCHER

Any word can be used to begin this game. A full-sentence prompt could be used as well: "Think back over what we have learned this morning and formulate a one-minute talk about something that stands out in your mind." This sentence serves as an excellent tool for summarization. (The length of time varies, depending on class size or team size.) Groups could also compile their notes to produce a written summary.

DISCUSSION QUESTIONS

19

QUALITY IN/QUALITY OUT

OBJECTIVE

To help participants recognize that **excellence in the output depends on excellence in the input**

TIME

Approximately 15 minutes

MATERIALS

Transparency 19-1

MINILECTURE

Psychologists tell us the average person needs to hear a new concept four or five times before the idea sinks in and is remembered. Effective leaders tell their followers, collectively and individually, over and over about the importance of their mission. Their dialogs do not resemble that described by Joe Kapp, former Vikings quarterback: "The longest dialogue I ever had with Bud [Grant, Vikings coach, 1967-1985] was a monologue, and it lasted three words—'Get a haircut.'"

Assuming that people understand directions after hearing them only once often leads to errors and confusion. Errors and confusion lead to poor morale, lost time, wasted efforts and unnecessary expense. To illustrate, I am going to ask that you perform a task today. There will be two groups. The first will receive the instructions only once. The second will be given the instructions more than once. Because the first group will not have an input of the highest quality, their output will probably not be of the highest quality. The second group should demonstrate a higher-quality output. You will have 10 minutes to complete your assignment.

STEPS TO FOLLOW

1. Divide the class into two groups. After giving the following instructions to both groups, send the first group to a breakout room and have them return in 10 minutes.

2. Give these instructions: *I'd like you as a group to think of at least five different desks that creatively represent five different people. For example this desk [show Transparency 19-1 now] might belong to Steven Spielberg, creator of Jurassic Park. Please get started now. Please do not ask me to repeat the instructions.*

3. Take an extra *few* minutes with the remaining group to restate the assignment, to ask if they have questions, and to give a few additional examples:

> Two desks facing each other but having only one chair in the middle could belong to Siamese twins

> A desk with a chair, with its arms in slings, could belong to an orthopedic surgeon.

A desk with a top that opens like a coffin might belong to Dracula.

A desk with size 22 athletic shoes on the legs might belong to Shaquille O'Neal.

Encourage them to relax, have fun, be as creative as possible. Also tell them that, in the interest of time, it might be best for them to work individually for the next five or six minutes and then to discuss their results as a team.

4. Have the teams compare their answers and discuss the following questions.

DISCUSSION QUESTIONS

✓ On a scale of 1 to 10, how would you evaluate the quality of your team's output?

✓ What would the result have been if the instructor had repeated the directions or had offered several other examples or had encouraged the first group, expressing confidence in their ability to complete the task?

✓ Can you think of a situation where, paradoxically, the very lack of equal treatment was a sufficient prompt for excellence to emerge?

✓ What are some of the reasons why people issue instructions only once in the workplace?

✓ What are some of the reasons why the recipients of those instructions fail to ask for clarification?

✓ What is the nature of the instructions you typically receive?

✓ What is the nature of the instructions you typically give?

20

COMPLAIN AND EXPLAIN

OBJECTIVE   To identify the components of **good communications between supplier and process owner**

TIME   Approximately 15 minutes

MATERIALS   Handout 20-1: Winput, one for each participant; Flip chart and marking pens if Game Stretcher is done

MINILECTURE   *We cannot assume we know what our suppliers expect of us. Nor should the suppliers assume they know what we expect of them. The only way for us to clarify expectations is to talk to one another, to complain if need be. If the quality of the input being provided you by your supplier is less than you feel it should be, you have a responsibility to speak to the supplier, to make your needs clear. Similarly, it is important that you permit suppliers to explain what they require from you. (You are the customer at this stage, accepting an output, which becomes your input, the beginning of your process.) Henry Ford II's dictum, "Never complain, never explain" is certainly not applicable in a Quality workplace.*

   Today, I'd like you to work with one other person and imagine two dialogs between the supplier and the process owner. In the first dialog on this worksheet [distribute the Winput handout now], you will depict a dialog that shows a positive exchange. In the second dialog, you will show a negative exchange between the supplier and the process owner. To get you started, you may wish to think about a typical day at work. Some input is placed in your in-basket. Typically, the person who placed it there or who handed it to you is your supplier. Before you can transform that input in your in-basket to an output for your out-basket, you have to engage in some work, some process to create a service or product that can be delivered to your customer.

   Think about an exchange that might be conducted between the supplier to your process and you as the process owner. First write a short script for an ideal exchange. Then create a script for a less than ideal exchange between a supplier and the process owner.

STEPS TO FOLLOW   **1.** Have participants work in dyads.
   2. Distribute Handout 20-1.
   3. After 10 or 15 minutes, have dyads exchange their scripts.

DISCUSSION QUESTIONS

✓ When is the last time you explained to a supplier exactly what you needed from him/her?

✓ Did you give the person an opportunity to explain what he/she needed from you?

✓ Does your firm have an annual supplier conference? If so, what have you learned from it?

✓ If not, could you help arrange one?

✓ Your suppliers view you as their customer. When is the last time they asked you how satisfied you are with the product or services they are supplying to you?

✓ How can complaining to a supplier help improve quality?

GAME STRETCHER

(15 minutes) Ask for a volunteer to collect all the worksheets and to prepare on the flip chart a list of the ingredients necessary to open exchanges between the supplier and the process owner. (*Note:* This is a challenging assignment, for the volunteer has to analyze *between the lines* and determine what unwritten techniques were employed in the exchanges to make them effective or ineffective. The list can be posted in the classroom and then later shared with other employees via electronic mail or the company newsletter.)

WINPUT

Write a 10- to 20-line script depicting an ideal communication between the supplier to a process and the owner of the process.

Now write a 10- to 20-line script, using the same illustration, to show a communication effort between supplier and process owner that does not succeed.

OVERVIEW: OUTPUT

The process is designed to have an end product. This product does not sit on our desks for six months; it is delivered to an end user or customer. We are all suppliers to someone else's process and we are all customers *of* someone else's process. You as the process owner have a number of important considerations involving the processes you engage in. Not only are you expected to do excellent work and to produce a high-quality product, you are also expected to ask your customers from time to time how satisfied they are with the product they are receiving from you. You are also expected to communicate your expectations to your supplier from time to time.

In addition, as a Quality proponent, you are expected to continuously seek ways to improve the processes of your work. This means thinking critically about every single step of every single process you engage in, and asking yourself if those steps are all necessary. What steps can be combined or streamlined? Which are costing too much or contain too many errors? Which parts of the process are customers complaining about the most? Where are the bottlenecks? The inefficiencies? The absurdities?

It helps to draw a flow diagram of your work processes and to compare the actual flow diagram to an ideal flow diagram, to determine where the process is not operating as it should. Dr. Joseph Juran, a Quality guru, advises us to compare how the process is actually performing to how the process is *capable* of performing. The actual and ideal flow diagrams help us understand where improvement is needed.

By the time you have finished flow diagramming all your processes and by the time everyone else in your organization has finished his or hers, it's time to examine them all over again. You can see why the Quality movement is referred to as one of continuous improvement.

21

SUMO FOR YOU?

OBJECTIVE

To illustrate the **many aspects of excellence in a process**

TIME

Approximately 20 minutes

MATERIALS

Flip chart/paper; two large stars (gold, if possible); marking pens; masking tape

MINILECTURE

In Kaizen, author Masaaki Imai talks about the sumo tournaments in Japan. Wrestlers in these national sports events may receive one of three awards in addition to the tournament championship award: an outstanding performance award, a skill awards, and a fighting spirit award. Even if a wrestler loses the match, he might still win the fighting spirit award, symbolizing the importance of effort. The process is emphasized more than the product or ultimate outcome.

As a team, you will be asked to list as many Quality-related words as possible for each letter in the word process. Here is a sheet of chart paper [distribute one to each team]. Write the letter p on the top of the left side. Beneath it write the r. Continue to write the word process vertically.

Now, I'd like you to write as many Quality-related words as you can think of, beginning with the letter p. Product might be one example. Then write as many as you can think of beginning with the letter r. Recognition might be one such word. And so on. You'll have 15 minutes.

STEPS TO FOLLOW

1. Appoint one person as judge. He/she will not join either team.

2. Divide the class into teams of five or six.

3. Distribute chart paper and marking pens.

4. Allow 15 minutes for the exercise.

5. Have the teams tally how many words they had. The judge gives the first star award to the team with the most words. (The judge tapes the star to the chart paper.) Then the judge posts each team's work along one wall and decides which team had the most *relevant* Quality-related words. He or she tapes the star to the paper representing the highest quality (as opposed to the first award, given for the highest quantity).

6. As the judge is deciding, ask each team to select the one word from their list they feel is most representative of Quality and to explain why they think it is so.

✓ What criteria, other than speed, determine customer satisfaction with the output of a process?

✓ In what ways are employees' contributions recognized in your organization? In what other ways *could* their contributions be recognized?

✓ If we relate the fighting spirit, outstanding performance, and skill awards from sumo contests to our education system, what other recognition (beyond sports and academic honor rolls) could schools give students?

GAME STRETCHER

(5–15 minutes) This activity could be used with any word that depicts an aspect of Quality.

22

SMART CHARTS

OBJECTIVE

To introduce the basic components of a **flow diagram**

TIME

Approximately 20 minutes

MATERIALS

Transparency 22-1: Flowchart Symbols; copies of Handout 22-1: TQM Tool: Flowchart

MINILECTURE

Flowcharting is not hard. Listen to the simplicity with which Dr. Deming described it: "Draw a flow diagram. Who's your customer? What comes in? What goes out? Do you know your customer? Do you know what he needs? Almost nobody does≡ "

For flowcharting, you need only five symbols to indicate progression through the process. Begin with an oval to indicate input. Then skip immediately to the right-hand bottom of the page and draw another oval to indicate output. Do this before you begin filling in the process steps to ensure staying on track.

Next, use a rectangle to indicate steps in the process, and a line to connect the oval to the rectangle and the rectangle to the next step. Sometimes we reach a decision point, indicated by a diamond. The decision point is a question, answerable by yes or no. If the answer is yes, what do we do next? If the answer is no, what do we do next?

Occasionally, we need a circle to show a delay in the process. We may need to wait for approval or we may have to wait for data from another department before we can continue our own process.

STEPS TO FOLLOW

1. Divide the class into small groups.

2. Show Transparency 22-1.

3. Distribute Handout 22-1. Explain that it represents a deliberately simple process, that of using a typewriter to address an envelope. Give them a few minutes to study the diagram and then have them discuss how and where improvements could be made. Also ask them to consider what data would need to be collected.

Typical questions would be these:

> Is it better to collect all the envelopes and type them all at once or to type them individually as they are needed?

> Is it worth obtaining a postage meter to keep in the office, rather than going to the post office or mail room for mailing?

How often are mistakes made? How much do they cost to fix? (Time is money.) Is it worth sending the typist to a typing class?

Is it worth having preprinted address labels?

Is it cost-effective to purchase window envelopes?

Should a computer database be established?

4. Have the groups share their observations.

DISCUSSION QUESTIONS

✓ How many of your processes have you already flowcharted?

✓ What are you doing differently as a result of your analyses?

✓ If you have not yet begun to flowchart, what is preventing you?

✓ Which processes in which you engage most need improvement?

✓ Whom would you like to have on a team to improve these processes?

FLOWCHART SYMBOLS

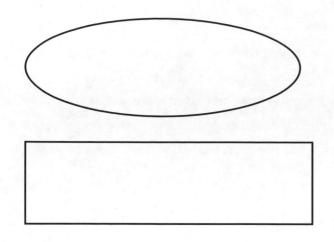

Oval = the start of a process (input) and end of a process (output)

Rectangle = a step in the process

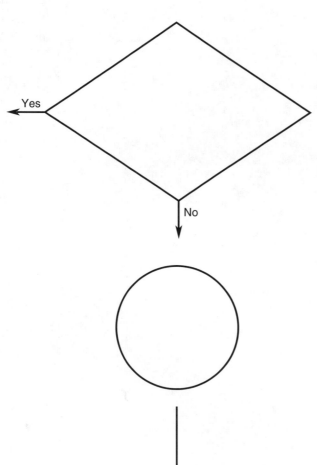

Diamond = a decision point (a question answerable by yes or no)

Circle = a waiting period

Line (arrow) = a link between steps of the process

TQM TOOL: FLOWCHART

Here is a flow diagram of a simple process—addressing an envelope by using a typewriter. As you study it, see if you can think of ways the process might be made more efficient.

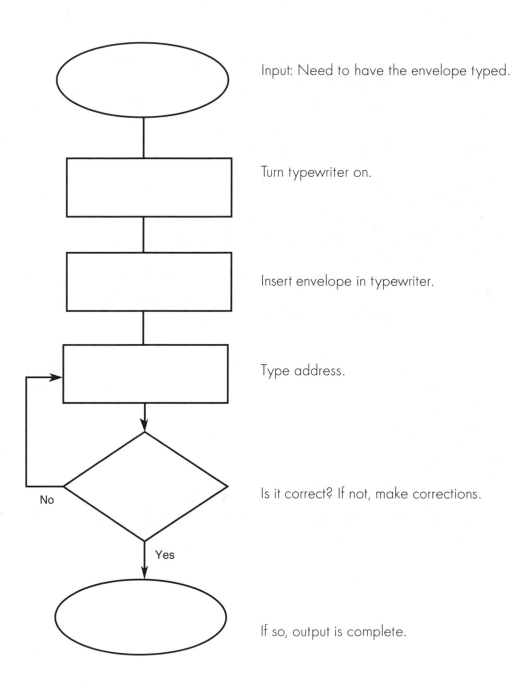

Input: Need to have the envelope typed.

Turn typewriter on.

Insert envelope in typewriter.

Type address.

Is it correct? If not, make corrections.

If so, output is complete.

23

WARTS AND ALL

OBJECTIVE

To develop the understanding via **flowcharting** that different people may perform the same **process** in different ways

TIME

Approximately 25 minutes

MATERIALS

Five sheets of chart paper; marking pens; masking tape

MINILECTURE

Depicting exactly how we perform a given process may reveal "warts" in the process. But that is why we go through such analysis—in the belief that we are not perfect, the organization is not perfect, the process is not perfect. "By studying these charts you can often uncover loopholes which are potential sources of trouble," the editors of GOAL/QPC's The Memory Jogger tell us. Only by getting down on paper the actual steps in the process and then examining those steps can we hope to improve them. (The major tasks of teams is to improve processes; that is why in many organizations, the teams are called "process action teams.")

Even though you may have done a given process for years, even though you know it upside down and inside out, there may still be room for improvement. Sometimes, simply by talking with other process owners we learn things that they are doing and that we could be doing. In other words, five different people could be performing the same process in five different ways. The trick is to learn which parts of which processes are the most effective and then to incorporate them into a standardized process, which could still be a candidate for further improvement.

Today, I'm going to have five teams flowchart the same process—the process of getting up in the morning and getting dressed. The "output" will be a completely dressed individual, walking out the door. The "customer" for this output will usually be the boss, who will take this output and use it as input to begin a number of work processes that must be completed today.

Remember to start with an oval to indicate input—what starts the process. Move immediately to the bottom right-hand side of the page and show the oval for output. Then go back and fill in the steps between the two ovals, using a rectangle to show action or a step in the process and a diamond to show you have reached a decision point. (The decision points are written as questions, answerable by yes or no.)

STEPS TO FOLLOW

1. Divide the class into five groups. Distribute chart paper and marking pens. As a team, they should depict the steps involved in the process of getting dressed in the morning.

2. Walk around to ensure they have written input and output first, before they begin depicting the steps. *Note:* This activity generates a lot of laughter as they realize—very soon—that, while they all engage in the same process, they don't all do it the same way. Even the first entry of input demonstrates this. For some, the input is the alarm going off, and the supplier (the one who set the alarm) is oneself. For others, no alarm clock is needed; they have an internal alarm clock. Some may have a biological need that awakens them. For others, it may be an animal needing to be fed or needing to be walked (the animal supplies the input). Still others may have a newborn child, whose cries are the only alarm they need. Others may have spouses who awaken them.

The point of all this is to relate it to the workplace. Although several people may be doing the same processes, they may be doing them differently. The warts in one person's process can be removed and replaced by an efficiency in another person's process. Perhaps the wart can even be eliminated.

3. Provide help as needed. When the charts are completed, post and have the teams *briefly* explain theirs and compare them to the others.

DISCUSSION QUESTIONS

✓ What did you learn from this activity?

✓ How can this knowledge be transported to the workplace?

✓ Why might some employees be reluctant to depict their work?

✓ What could you do to encourage them, to drive out their fears?

✓ If employees are performing a process wrong, what may be causing them to do so?

✓ Where will people find time to flowchart all their processes?

✓ In addition to discovering warts, what other purpose can flow diagrams serve?

OVERVIEW: VALUE-ADDED STEPS

Sam Walton, founder of Wal-Mart stores, encouraged his employees to "eliminate the dumb." This simple but effective philosophy lies behind the push in the Quality movement to eliminate from a process the steps that do not add value. A helpful question as we scrutinize the work we do is this: If my customers could see what I am doing right now, would they be willing to pay me to do it?

In some organizations, for example, eight signatures of approval are required for a single document. Each signature supersedes the signature that precedes it. The ultimate signature is the truly authorizing one. Are all those signatures really required? What is the cost of such duplicated effort?

As we examine the steps in a flow diagram, we must simultaneously ask whether each step is really needed. Could this step be combined with another? What value does this step add to the final product? As the team scrutinizes the sequence of the process, they may come to ask if the process *itself* is necessary. Such questions indicate an organization's total commitment to the continuous improvement of processes. They also indicate commitment to the customer or end user. Teams looking at end products for end users need to ask,

Are customers satisfied with what we are giving them? How do we know? (Remember that, without backup data, you're just another person with an opinion.)

Are we giving customers some things that they don't even want?

Are we *not* giving customers some things that they *do* want?

Tough questions have to be asked as we determine what adds value. But, without tough questions and tough decisions based on the answers to those questions, we may be losing customers. Losing customers ultimately leads to losing jobs.

24

BEAUTY AND THE LEAST

OBJECTIVE

To encourage consideration of work processes by asking the question, Is this a **value-added step**?

TIME

Approximately 5 minutes

MATERIALS

None

MINILECTURE

Ray Kroc, founder of the tremendously successful McDonald's, swore that he could see beauty in a hamburger bun. And while cynics and sophisticates may snicker at his unbridled passion for the products he offered customers, the truth remains that Kroc was richer than most of us can dream of being.

I'd like you to think, seriously, about the aspects of your job that you most enjoy doing, the aspects that would be equivalent to Mr. Kroc's feelings about hamburgers. List four if you can. Then think about the parts of your job that you least enjoy, maybe even hate doing. Again, list four. [Pause] Now, I'd like you to go back and indicate the importance of all eight items in terms of customer satisfaction. Use a scale of 1 to 5, with 5 being most important to the customer who will receive your output. [Pause] When you have finished that, do one last thing: Indicate with a star the one item you spend the majority of your time on.

STEPS TO FOLLOW

1. Have participants list their items and assess them.

2. If time permits, ask for a volunteer to share his or her insights.

DISCUSSION QUESTIONS

✓ Do the things you love doing occupy more time than the things you hate doing, or is it the other way around?

✓ How can we increase the time spent on the few vital aspects of our work and decrease the time spent on the many trivial aspects?

GAME STRETCHER

(10 minutes) Use the same process but define importance in other ways—in terms of the cost-effectiveness, senior management, OSHA, the union, regulations, the environment, etc.

25

VALUE THE VALUE-ADDED

OBJECTIVE   To expose participants to value analysis: the process of determining the value of **micro-** and **macroprocesses**

TIME   Approximately 1 hour

MATERIALS   Chart paper; marking pens; masking tape; copies of Handout 25-1: School Daze, one for each participant

MINILECTURE   *"What is the point of doing something very efficiently that should not be done at all?"* asks management guru Peter Drucker. Keeping his question in mind, we are going to examine a process that is familiar to each of us—schooling. Even if you do not have a child in school, you're familiar with the schooling process because, without it, you would not be sitting in this room today. We are going to ask probing questions about that process and the value of its components in relation to the purpose of the process. The questions may trouble you or make you uncomfortable but having your mental waters troubled is a sure sign that you are thinking about situations in a new way.

Ideally, the approach you use with your group today is the approach you will use when you return to the office or shop floor and begin to examine your work processes. Let's begin by having you think about a typical day in the life of an elementary school child. If no one in your group has a child in school, think back to your own school days. The macroprocesses in which you engaged are broad, generalized processes, such as learning to communicate better. A microprocess is a subset of the macroprocess, a process such as learning to spell or learning to write an essay.

As a team, I'd like you to determine the five most valuable microprocesses that you engaged in as a school child (or the five most important your child engages in today). Start by brainstorming the macroprocesses and then writing microprocesses beneath each. Next, put a star beside the five microprocesses the team feels are most important. Transfer those onto another sheet of chart paper.

STEPS TO FOLLOW   1. Form teams of 6 to 8 participants. Distribute chart paper and marking pens. Appoint a leader whose primary responsibility is to ensure the team comes up with five microprocesses within a 20- to 25-minute period. The processes (a series of sequential steps leading to clear output) begin with the *macro* (such as learning about other countries) and become more detailed or *micro* (such as writing a report on a book about Japan, watching a film about Africa, or writing to a foreign pen pal). (*Note:* Save these lists; you may wish to use them in activity 27.)

2. Have them write a macroprocess and beneath it, their five most valuable microprocesses on chart paper. Post the papers around the room.

3. Distribute Handout 25-1, then circulate among the teams to see if they need assistance.

4. After 20 to 25 minutes, call on the spokesperson from each group to share answers to the final two questions on the handout.

GAME STRETCHER

(10-20 minutes) Go through the same procedure of determining the value of macro- and microprocesses related to work functions.

SCHOOL DAZE

Choose the one process from all those posted that *you* feel is the most valuable. _____

_____

Work with your team to decide on the most valuable process: (The team choice may differ from your selection.)

_____

Answer these questions:

1. As a team, you have selected the process you believe has the greatest value. How would you define "value"? Do you believe the education you received has value? Again, how would you define that value?

2. What is the purpose of an elementary school education?
   What should its outputs be?
   What is needed from the microprocess you selected?
   Why is it needed?
   What is the purpose behind this microprocess?
   How can we redesign that process to achieve the purpose we have identified?
   What price are we willing to pay?
   How would we redesign the macroprocess of educating a child today? What can be eliminated because it has little value (according to the definition you have given that word)?

3. Based on the questions you have answered and the discussion you held as you answered them, answer just two more questions and appoint a spokesperson to report on these last two questions:

   What did you learn from this exercise?
   How can it be applied to the work you do?

26

LEAVE YOUR VALUES AT THE FRONT DESK

OBJECTIVE
To encourage analysis of parts of a process and total **processes that lend value to functions** of an organization

TIME
Approximately 20 minutes

MATERIALS
Chart paper lists of macro- and microprocesses involved in education; additional chart paper; marking pens; masking tape; Transparency 26-1: Value Scale

MINILECTURE
Author Richard Lederer, while traveling in Europe, found a notice in hotel room, which read: "Please leave your values at the front desk." In a sense, we have to leave our personal values at the front desk if they conflict with organizational values. As we learned in an earlier activity, if we are creative by nature and so love doing the creative aspects of our job, we must minimize the time we spend on them if those aspects are not adding value for the customer.

We are going to use educational macro- and microprocesses to help us define which aspects of the learning process add the most value for the customer. A teacher's opinion of what is important may differ from a student's, from a parent's, from an employer's. What we in the workplace think is valuable may differ from what a potential customer thinks is valuable, as the following example shows:

> *A minister took his 50 cent purchase to the cashier in a small store before realizing he had no money with him. Half jokingly, he suggested that she could come hear him preach in return for the item. Then he noted, "But I'm afraid I don't have any sermons worth 50 cents."*

> *Trying to be helpful, the cashier offered a suggestion of her own: "Perhaps I could come to hear you twice."*

As a team, you will look at educational macro- and microprocesses and try to reach consensus on which numbers to ascribe to each of them. Use the scale on this transparency. [Show Transparency 26-1 now.]

STEPS TO FOLLOW
1. Post the macro- and microprocess lists from the preceding lesson, or have teams write down broad educational processes and the more specific microprocesses or means by which the macroprocesses are carried out. (Teams may prefer to examine the macroprocess, communicating, and the

various microprocesses by which organizations share information.) Pass out marking pens and chart paper.

2. Ask participants to join the same teams that worked on activity 25 or to form new teams if 25 was not done.

3. Show Transparency 26-1 and have them score as many of the items as possible during a 15-minute period. Teams can use *any* number between 1 and 10.

4. Have a spokesperson from each team give a report once the 15-minute period has elapsed.

DISCUSSION QUESTIONS

✓ What do parents expect of the educational function?

✓ What do students expect of the educational function?

✓ What do teachers expect of the educational function?

✓ What do prospective employers expect of the educational function?

✓ What happens when expectations from any one (or any combination) of these groups are not aligned with the mission? What happens when the expectations from various groups are dissimilar?

✓ Are each of your work processes aligned with the organizational mission?

✓ How can you be sure the values you attach to work processes are the same values your customers hold?

✓ How can we achieve greater congruency among the expectations of various groups?

GAME STRETCHER

(10-20 minutes) Use the same process to assess the value of a work function(s).

VALUE SCALE

<u>10</u> = Imperative, required by internal or external regulations

<u>8</u> = Integral to organizational mission

<u>6</u> = Important, with definite value

<u>4</u> = Indirect value, barely recognized by customer

<u>2</u> = Inconsequential, could be omitted and no one would ask for it

<u>0</u> = Impossible to justify as having any value at all

SECTION 4

THE PROCESS OWNER

Many people are drawn to the Quality movement because of its democratic nature. Just as it turns pyramids upside down to place managers in a supportive role, it also places workers at the top. It acknowledges that the role of the worker is different from, but equal in importance to, the role of the manager. It has not always been true in American business that process owners were recognized as experts in their spheres. Nor have process owners always been invited to participate in making decisions regarding their spheres.

Generally speaking, the people who are closest to the work know the work best. Their input is critical if the processes of their work are truly to be improved.

Games to develop empowerment, enhance recognition, and increase open book management efforts are presented in this section.

OVERVIEW: EMPOWERING THE WORKER

The word *empowerment* has been bandied about so much that it has lost some of the excitement it once conveyed. Nonetheless, if a Quality focus is to permeate an organization, then its employees need access to some of the decision making power that once resided in the hands of managers alone. To empower employees does not mean to relinquish all authority. Rather, it means to share the power—granting to capable employees the delegated right to make certain decisions regarding the work they perform.

Empowerment, too, requires mind shifts on the parts of managers and employees alike. Managers of the past may have believed that knowledge was power and that their particular power was derived from the knowledge they possessed. There was often an unwillingness to share knowledge. With the advent of philosophies such as open book management, today's manager realizes more and more the benefits to be derived from employee involvement and decision making at the lowest possible levels. Informed employees are usually more involved and more committed to organizational goals.

Some employees actually prefer to be micromanaged. (After all, such a management style means employees don't have to think—they only have to do what they are told and so the risks are diminished, as is the possibility of making a mistake.) For such individuals, a new thinking is necessary, one that embraces change and the idea that all employees can be agents of change.

The changes wrought by empowerment require more and more careful communication between supervisor and employee. There must be a delineation of the tasks the newly empowered employee is expected to undertake. Accompanying this delineation should be discussion of the level of authority the employee has in the execution of the task.

27

CIRCLE OF POWER

OBJECTIVE

To promote discussion of the degree of **empowerment** participants feel they possess

TIME

Approximately 10 minutes

MATERIALS

None

MINILECTURE

I'd like you to draw a circle on a clean sheet of paper. Label it M, since the circle represents you in your organization. [Pause] Next, draw a circle to represent your boss and label it B. [Pause] The final circle will represent or symbolize the organization for which you work. Write the letter O near the circle.

Amateur psychologists like to engage in simple tests that may reveal new insights into an individual's persona. This is one such test. Whether or not it provides deep psychological insights, it is bound to stimulate some good discussion. It is one of many ways that we can—formally or informally—learn more about ourselves. To quote Plato: "The life which is unexamined is not worth living."

Let's take a look now at what we have and see if there is any connection between the symbolic and the real, as far as empowerment is concerned. Did anyone have an M circle the same size as the B circle? If so, it is likely you have been given a considerable amount of authority and empowerment in your organization. Is this so?

Did anyone have all three circles the same size? This would suggest a real partnership, with each element contributing equally. If the circles were concentric, with M in the innermost circle and O in the outer circle, you have a good sense of the big picture and of systemic relationships. If your M circle is bigger than your B circle, you just may have more power than your boss does.

STEPS TO FOLLOW

1. Have participants draw circles and then encourage them to develop their own half serious interpretations.

2. Have participants share their interpretations with one another. If any are especially clever, ask permission to post them around the room.

DISCUSSION QUESTIONS

✓ What do you know about the Rorschach test and how it operates?

✓ Are you familiar with the work of Harvard professor David McClelland, who uses a thematic apperception test to help people understand their motivational drives?

✓ Other than this lighthearted effort to have us consider empowerment, what else about your speech and/or behavior might reveal the degree of empowerment you possess?

GAME STRETCHER

(10-15 minutes) After you have done some reading about McClelland's use of pictures to reveal the need for power, the need for achievement and the need for affiliation, you may wish to show participants a picture, have them write a brief story concerning it, and then discuss with them what the stories reveal in terms of power, achievement, and affiliation.

28

A QUESTION OF LEARNING

OBJECTIVE   To raise questions as a prelude to **learning**

TIME   Approximately 10 minutes

MATERIALS   None

MINILECTURE   *Dr. Deming said, "Without a theory, there are no questions. And without questions, there is no learning. Hence, without a theory, there is no learning." The game in which you will soon engage is not profound. However, it will raise some questions, that may ultimately evolve into a theory.*

I am going to mention a category—such as movie star. You will take the first person who pops into your head and then write three adjectives to describe that image. For example, "movie star" may have led you to think of Elizabeth Taylor. The three adjectives to describe her might be elegant, rich, and popular. If you are ready, here are the four categories. Again, you will allow one example of the word to pop into your head and then you will write three adjectives to describe the image in your head.

The first category is color. What color comes into your head and how would you describe that color? Use three adjectives. [Pause.] The second category is animal. What animal comes into your head first? Describe that animal with three adjectives. [Pause.] The third category is modes of transportation. What is the first image that comes to mind to show how people or things are transported? Describe that image with three adjectives. [Pause] Finally, the category is places where water is found. What image of water comes into your head? Describe it.

STEPS TO FOLLOW

1. Have participants write three adjectives to describe each noun that popped into their heads.

2. Share the amateur psychologist's interpretation (pausing after each to allow laughter to build and erupt): "The words you wrote for 1 (the first color that popped into your head) are supposed to reveal how you feel about yourself. The words you wrote for 2 (the first animal that popped into your head) reveal how others perceive you ≡ or how you *think* they perceive you. The words you wrote for 3 (the first vehicle that pops into your head) may reveal the level of empowerment you have reached. And the words you wrote for 4 (the first image of water that pops into your head) usually reveal your attitudes toward sex."

✓ What 10 words would you use to describe your work? What 10 words would your co-workers use? Your boss? Your customers?

✓ How empowered do you feel you are in the work you do? Would your boss have a similar perception of the degree of empowerment you possess (or believe you possess)? If not, how could the two perceptions be made more aligned?

✓ What causes the differences in the perceptions we have of ourselves and the perceptions others hold?

✓ How can we reduce the differences between what we regard as high quality and what our customers might consider high quality?

GAME STRETCHER

(10 minutes) Ask if anyone in the class has a favorite amateur psychologist game of his or her own. If so, take a few minutes to explore it with the class.

29

INVERTING PYRAMIDS

OBJECTIVE   To illustrate that the **inverted pyramid**, with managers supporting teams and process owners, can be achieved relatively easily

TIME   Approximately 10 minutes

MATERIALS   Transparencies 29-1: Traditional Pyramid and 29-2: Inverted Pyramid; optional prize for the first person to solve the problem

MINILECTURE   *Change is often better received when those affected realize how important it is to change and how easy it can be. "When you're through changing," Bruce Barton comments, "you're through." Many organizations have found the conversion to TQM not as difficult as they had first anticipated. To illustrate the fact that radical change can sometimes be accomplished with little disruption, I'd like you to look at this diagram of the traditional organizational structure—with the CEO at the top and the various layers beneath, all supporting the top.*

With the advent of TQM, that pyramid is often inverted: Senior management becomes a base or foundation to support the teams at the top, which are engaged in the work of continuous improvement. My question to you is this: Can you change the familiar pyramid to an inverted pyramid in only three moves of the circles shown here?

STEPS TO FOLLOW   **1.** Show Transparency 29-1 and ask if someone—in only three circle moves—can completely invert the pyramid.

2. After about 5 minutes, if no one has figured it out, show the Inverted Pyramid transparency. If someone *has* figured it out, have him or her show the answer to the class. Award the prize, and then show the Inverted Pyramid transparency.

DISCUSSION QUESTIONS   ✓ Other than the inverted pyramid, what other changes have you noticed in the workplace in the last five or ten years?

✓ How does today's manager differ from yesterday's? Today's leader? Today's worker?

✓ As your organization underwent its transformation to Quality, what aspects of the transformation were fairly easy to implement?

✓ Given the fact that the number of cellular telephone subscribers in 1983 was zero and in 1993 it was 16 million, what other technological advances will affect the way we work?

GAME STRETCHER

(10-15 minutes) Have participants discuss some of the new shapes that organizations are taking, such as the "pepperoni pizza" and the "shamrock." Then have them brainstorm additional shapes that organizations might take in the future.

TRADITIONAL PYRAMID

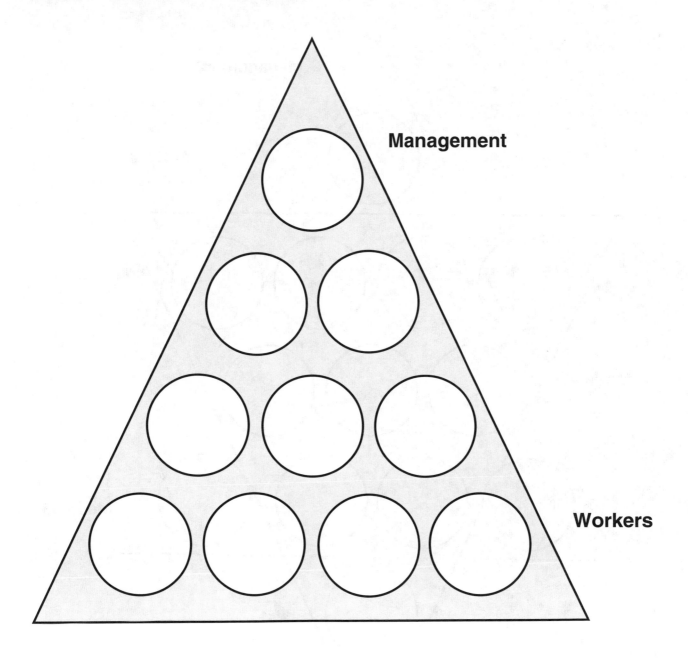

Management

Workers

INVERTED PYRAMID

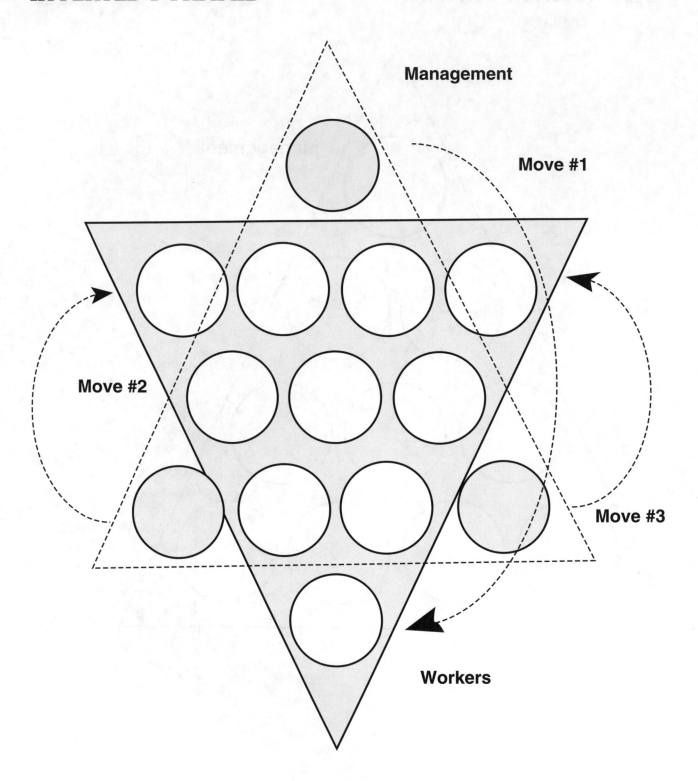

OVERVIEW: RECOGNIZING EMPLOYEE CONTRIBUTIONS

In far too many organizations, employees are not tapping the potential they possess. Often, they do not even realize what they possess until circumstances arise to bring out the best in them. (As Oliver Wendell Holmes wisely observed, "What lies behind us and what lies before us are nothing compared to what lies within us.")

It takes leadership to call forth the best in people. Just as Dr. Juran advises us to distinguish between actual process performance and process capability, so too must employees be given the circumstances that permit discovery of their capacity.

Once the organization learns of the innovation, the diligence, the productivity, and the improvements that individual employees and team members can effect, the organization is duty bound to recognize and reward their efforts.

But how does the organization learn such things? Further, how does it learn what *employees* consider appropriate and/or adequate reward? As is often the case, we need only ask questions and truly listen to the answers given. Assumptions have to be put aside.

For example, it is an incorrect assumption on the part of many managers that monetary rewards motivate employees to do better work and to become more involved. Research, particularly that of Frederick Herzberg, shows the fallacy of such thinking. To the surprise of most managers, employees prefer to be involved, to be given challenging work, and to have visible manifestations that they are valued by the organization.

Fortunately, the rewards that most employees seek are inexpensive. They take the form of respect and appreciation and invitations to participate. Whether we recognize the efforts of the individual or the team, the management staff—with minimal exertion of time, effort, and ingenuity—can discover what is important to employees. Armed with such discovery, the next step is easy.

30

WHY IS A MANHOLE ROUND?

OBJECTIVE

To stress the importance of having a vehicle by which **employee suggestions** are heard

TIME

Approximately 5 minutes

MATERIALS

Optional prize for the person who figures out the answer to the question

MINILECTURE

"Innovation," asserts John Scully, "has never come through bureaucracy and hierarchy. It's always come from individuals." Employee contributions can be recognized only if there is a vehicle and an environment that permit the free flow of ideas upwards.

There is a puzzle that relates to the need to have a close fit between the expression of ideas and their acknowledgment by upper management. There will be a prize for the first person who can figure it out: Why is a manhole round?

STEPS TO FOLLOW

1. Ask the question and allow a few minutes for participants to figure out the answer, which is, if the manhole were any other shape, the manhole cover could fall through the opening.

2. If someone figures it out, award the prize. If there is no correct answer, share the answer, then move along to the discussion questions, which encourage consideration of ways to prevent good ideas from falling between the cracks.

DISCUSSION QUESTIONS

✓ What suggestion program exists in your place of work?

✓ How could it be improved so that employee ideas do not fall through the cracks?

✓ Have you done any benchmarking to learn about suggestion programs in other organizations?

✓ If microchips are doubling in performance power every 18 months, what do you think is the rate for individuals (of both intellectual and actual performance power)?

31

CONTINUOUS IMPROVEMENT POSSIBILITIES

OBJECTIVE
To illustrate the concept of **continuous improvement**

TIME
Approximately 15 minutes

MATERIALS
None

MINILECTURE
"The measure of success is not whether you have a tough problem to deal with, but whether it's the same problem you had last year." John Foster Dulles' words reflect one of the cornerstones of the Quality movement: continuously moving forward, continuously improving.

Working in small groups, you will brainstorm as long a list as possible of ways to recognize employee contributions. In the spirit of continuous improvement, you should try to list things not already being done. Or, if they are being done, tell how they could be improved on.

STEPS TO FOLLOW
1. Form large groups of six to eight participants.

2. Announce that the groups will have 5 minutes to prepare their lists.

3. When the time is up, call on a each group to share their favorite idea. (*Note:* This selection of the favorite idea can become time-consuming. If they have not agreed on one idea within a minute, ask them to select any good idea.)

4. Next announce that they will now engage in the same exercise, but this time they will have one less person and only 4 minutes. The person who is now removed from their team serves as observer and makes a report to the team when the task has been completed. The task is to compile as long a list as they can—without any repeats—of ways to improve the employee recognition system.

DISCUSSION QUESTIONS
✓ How many workable ideas were generated in 5 (and in 4) minutes?

✓ How did the team respond when asked to do more with less?

32

IT'S NO FIB: IT'S FIBONACCI

OBJECTIVE	To show that contributions are based on **teamwork**
TIME	Approximately 10 minutes
MATERIALS	Transparency 32-1; optional prize for the winner
MINILECTURE	*"You seldom accomplish very much by yourself. You must get the assistance of others,"* Henry J. Kaiser asserted. This is what teamwork is all about—the workplace partnerships that allow us to add to what has already been contributed and to know that others will continue to add in the relentless search for excellence.

A thirteenth century Italian mathematician contributed today's game. It's called a Fibonacci. (If you already know what it is, please do not participate in this game.) The Fibonacci asks you to figure out what will be the next number in this sequence. [Show transparency.] |

STEPS TO FOLLOW

1. Show transparency.
2. Allow time for them to figure out the answer, which is that every number is the combined result of the preceding two numbers. So the next number in the sequence is 34.

DISCUSSION QUESTIONS

✓ What parallels can you draw between the Fibonacci and the work we do in organizations?

✓ How has the work you do been made more efficient because of someone else's contribution?

✓ What contribution have you made to improve efficiency?

✓ What accomplishments in your organization's history were the result of preceding efforts? In America's history? In world history?

✓ How can we develop within the workplace the feeling of cohesion, the belief that one's work is important to the work of others?

0,

   1,

      1,

         2,

            3,

               5,

                  8,

                     13,

                        21,

                           <u>?</u>

OVERVIEW: OPEN BOOK MANAGEMENT

Some managers feel that knowledge is power and that, the more knowledge they have (and keep to themselves), the more power they have. Open book managers reflect the antithesis of such thinking. They work to improve the good of the whole, not to increase their own turf. When Dr. Juran advises us to "eliminate turf wars," he speaks to the negative results of self-aggrandizement and department aggrandizement. The short-term results may seem warranted but the long-term effects seldom are.

A sense of interdependence pervades the modern workplace. When employees are given a chance to literally look at the books—a chance to understand the financial rationale behind most corporate policies—they can participate in executing policies with a greater sense of ownership. They can also evaluate better the factors that impinge on the decisions they are required to make.

The open book management style of sharing information does not always function in a formal, prescribed fashion. It always, however, functions in an open fashion, with a constant goal: the improvement of the work situation. Whether the data are written or orally presented, they are timely, relevant, and rational in the sense that they lend insight to the work employees are expected to do.

This philosophy represents a two-way flow of information—at every level of a Quality organization. We find, for example, members of a quality improvement team making a presentation to the Quality Council and seeking approval before proceeding to the next stage of their idea implementation. Employees of the past may have been given the Council's decision without ever learning the reasons for that decision. In the information embedded fabric of the modern organization, though, employees receive not only the decision but the explanation for it as well. The decision without the rationale does not allow team members to improve on their next submission.

Open book management does not promote the unnecessary flow of information. It *does* promote deep knowledge of the facts and figures related to decisions.

33

A GREAT GAME

OBJECTIVE	To familiarize participants with the concept of **open book management**
TIME	Approximately 20 minutes
MATERIALS	None
MINILECTURE	*"We are drowning in information but starved for knowledge," John Naisbitt observes. Similarly, Jack Stack, author of* The Great Game of Business *(Doubleday, 1992), proclaims, "Numbers are not a substitute for leadership. What's important is how you use them." Stack is a proponent of open book management, a philosophy that shares pertinent financial information with all employees. Throughout his book, Stack compares business to a game. I'd like you to probe that comparison further.*

STEPS TO FOLLOW

1. Form groups of four or five.

2. Have participants free association for 2 or 3 minutes regarding the business/game comparison. Then have them share their ideas with others in their group. Next, they will compile a master list of comparisons without duplicating one another's ideas.

3. They will eliminate from the list any words that do not pertain to games, and will then—using some or all of the words that remain—prepare a one-sentence statement comparing business to a game.

DISCUSSION QUESTIONS

✓ Jack Stack refers to scorecards that he feels every employee should have. What information do you think should be on such cards?

✓ Relate the quotations by Naisbitt and Stack to your own organization.

✓ Stack's aim is to have employees thinking like owners. What would it take in your organization for that kind of thinking to become standard?

GAME STRETCHER

(10 minutes) The free association technique can be used with any topic at any time but works especially well as a first hour icebreaker when groups are given words from the course title.

34

THERE'RE NUMBERS IN SAFETY

OBJECTIVE   To develop clear organizational **communication**

TIME   Approximately 10 minutes

MATERIALS   None

MINILECTURE   *"In the end," a Senegalese saying points out, "we will conserve only what we love. We will love only what we understand. We will understand only what we are taught." Open book management confirms this ancient wisdom: For the organization to be conserved, leaders must teach employees about, and develop understanding of, the factors that determine success and failure. In many organizations, management takes an active role in developing awareness of safety; workplace accidents and workplace violence are critical issues for most of us. Workmen's compensation cases alone cost companies about $18 billion each year.*

STEPS TO FOLLOW
1. Have participants brainstorm ways to celebrate the achievement of having reached 100,000 hours without a single workplace accident.

2. Form teams of six or seven members and ask them to share their ideas in the small groups.

3. Have one person from each team move to a new team to discuss the cost of workplace accidents–financial as well as emotional costs.

DISCUSSION QUESTIONS
✓ How would a leader use such numbers?

✓ What other numbers are important to employees?

✓ Are you using the numbers related to your work as a leader would use them?

✓ Do you know what you (and all other employees) are costing the firm (in terms of benefits, training, medical costs, health care, etc.)?

35

NEVER FOOL THE PLAYERS

OBJECTIVE

To reinforce the Quality concept that **people closest to the process usually know the process best**

TIME

Approximately 15 minutes

MATERIALS

None

MINILECTURE

Jack Stack maintains that "you can sometimes fool the fans, but you can never fool the players." What do you think he means by that?

[Allow a few minutes for discussion, touching upon the fact that the people closest to the process usually know the process best.]

Putting a fresh twist on an old saying often creates new insights about how we operate on a daily basis. We are going to attempt to do what Stack did with his fresh twist. Ideally, our words will be as meaningful as his.

STEPS TO FOLLOW

1. Have participants write down five to ten famous sayings, such as "You can fool some of the people some of the time≡ ." Then have them work in small groups of five or six.

2. They are to take one of the sayings and put a new spin on it, as Stack did with Lincoln's line. If time permits, have them explain how their version relates to the world of business.

DISCUSSION QUESTIONS

✓ It is altogether possible that you know your job better than your boss knows your job. That is because your boss's job is different from yours. What possible problems could arise from this fact?

✓ Can you relate Stack's comment to the business world?

✓ How can we increase the pride felt by workers who know their jobs better than anyone else in the company?

✓ How can we remove the blinders that workers who know their job better than anyone else in the company often put on themselves?

✓ How do we prevent expertise from turning into complacency?

SECTION **5**
CUSTOMER SATISFACTION

It all seems so simple: Without the customer, businesses will soon be *out* of business. You would think that satisfying the customer would be a pivotal operational goal. Yet, on a daily basis, those who serve the customer demonstrate rudeness, indifference, inefficiency, and a seeming disregard for customer needs.

Getting close to customers and determining what they expect are the driving forces behind the exercises in this section. By ascertaining what customers need and even by developing their awareness of what they need, we can better satisfy those on whom our jobs depend.

OVERVIEW:
GETTING CLOSE TO THE CUSTOMER

Customers may, of course, be inside or outside the organization. No matter where they are, however, we have an obligation to understand what they need and then to perfect products or services that meet those needs. There is a distinct danger in assuming we know what customers want. As reported in *Business Week* (August 8, 1994, p. 58),

> Rethinking quality can force some companies to abandon cherished beliefs. United Parcel Service Inc., for example, had always assumed that on-time delivery was the paramount concern of its customers. Everything else came second≡ . UPS even shaved the corners off delivery-van seats so drivers could slip out of their trucks more easily ≡ When UPS recently began asking broader questions about how it could improve service, it discovered that clients weren't as obsessed with on-time delivery as previously thought.

> The biggest surprise to UPS management: Customers wanted more interaction with drivers.

Charles Handy writes about living in an age of paradox, an age when contradiction rules our lives. Survival depends on making sense of the world, on resolving the contradictions. Like Sisyphus, we are pushing our private rocks of knowledge, which grow larger each day, up an incredibly tall mountain of public knowledge, which also grows larger each day. Inevitably, some of these knowledge pebbles collide and may even indent one another.

And so it is with Quality concepts regarding customer satisfaction. We cannot presume to know what customers want, but sometimes we need to educate customers about what they *should* want. In the words of Dr. Deming: "Moreover, the customer is not in a good position to prescribe product or service that will help him in the future."

Walking the tightrope between assuming and presuming requires great effort. Quality advocates, however, are willing to expend great effort to satisfy their customers.

One effort that has remarkable dividends for those seeking to understand their customers better is the focus group. Actual end users of the product or service are selected at random and brought into the organization for a brief meeting or series of meetings. Their input is actively sought and their ideas are acted on. The focus group idea is used with both internal and external customers.

36

THE CUSTOMER'S LAMENT: "I CAN'T GET NO SATISFACTION"

OBJECTIVE To sharpen awareness of actions **dissatisfied customers** may take

TIME Approximately 10 minutes

MATERIALS Chart paper; marking pens; masking tape

MINILECTURE *The now defunct Eastern airlines was famous for not satisfying its customers. In fact, "I hate Eastern" clubs were formed all over the United States by passengers and former passengers dissatisfied with the service provided. Those clubs were popular for more than 25 years.*

We sometimes underestimate the creativity and perseverance that dissatisfied customers can and do exhibit. Let's think a bit about the power customers really have, how we should respect that power, and how we can prevent problems by imagining them before they occur. Failure to do so can mean embarrassment and very expensive lessons. The possibility of such failure may explain why Jacques Maison-Rouge notes that "IBM always acts as if it were on the verge of losing every customer."

Before you begin, consider this example of John Barrier, whose story was reported in USA Today. Mr. Barrier walked into his bank in Spokane, Washington, one day, wearing construction clothes. After withdrawing $100, he went to get his parking ticket validated. The receptionist refused him, explaining that he had withdrawn money and to get free parking, he had to deposit money. He protested to the receptionist, pointing out that he was a substantial depositor at Old National Bank. She looked at him askance, as did the manager to whom he went to complain. Mr. Barrier next went to the bank headquarters, threatening to withdraw his money unless he received an apology from the manager in question. The next day, not having heard a word, Mr. Barrier returned to Old National and withdrew one million dollars.

If your customers are getting no satisfaction from you, they may take satisfaction in getting satisfaction beyond or above you!

Your assignment for the next 10 minutes is to list five things customers could, would, and/or should do to express their dissatisfaction. Try to think of some actions you yourself have taken. Think of actions you have read about others taking.

ANSWERS

The answers vary but typically you find: Lawsuits, complaints to the manager, protest marches, letters to the editor, articles or books describing bad customer experiences, boycotts, switching to another supplier, petitions, retaliation (refusing to pay a bill until satisfaction is received), press conferences, spreading the negative word about your organization or product to dozens of other people, contacting the Better Business Bureau or Nader's Raiders, contacting the local television station, open defiance, etc.

STEPS TO FOLLOW

1. Divide the class into small groups of two or three.

2. Have them make their lists. Allow about 10 minutes.

3. Ask for volunteers to share some of the more interesting or funny experiences.

DISCUSSION QUESTIONS

✓ Why are many employees bound by rules?

✓ How can empowerment prevent some customer complaints?

✓ As a customer, what are some of the expectations you have from those who provide you a service or product?

✓ What can we do to get close to customers before they get close to complaining?

GAME STRETCHER

(10–15 minutes) Ask participants to think specifically about their own customers and about actions those customers might take to express their concern or anger about the products or services being provided. Then ask them to spend time thinking about worst-case scenarios that might ensue and what can be done *now* to prevent such situations from arising.

37

DEFINE OR DECLINE

OBJECTIVE   To encourage taking the next step to define standards for both **satisfying the customer and supporting the mission**

TIME   Approximately 20 minutes

MATERIALS   Chart paper; marking pens; masking tape; Handout 37-1: How-to's for the What-to-do's, one for each participant

MINILECTURE   *Satisfying our customers should not be a complicated task, according to Lee Iacocca: "There's no great mystery to satisfying your customer. Build them a quality product and treat them with respect. It's that simple."*

There is some mystery, though. How do you define quality and respect? Let's take about 5 minutes now to have you work with a partner to define these two words.

STEPS TO FOLLOW   **1.** Have partners take 5 minutes to define the words. Then call on half the partner teams to share their definitions of quality and the other half to share their definitions of respect. In all likelihood, no two definitions will be the same, allowing you to continue the lecture.

MINILECTURE (CONTINUED)   *It's difficult—very difficult—to find an objective definition on which everyone can agree. Words, after all, are slippery things. They represent our subjective experiences and so it is often exasperating to try to achieve a common understanding. Imagine how difficult it is, then, for an organization to ask that everyone share in demonstrating words like quality and respect.*

One of the ways we can more closely align the implicit meaning of such words is to make explicit what we mean by them. For example, what does it mean to treat someone with respect? Does it mean not making fun of them? Does it mean not using profanity in their presence? Does it mean not insulting them? By defining the terms that we want to define our organization, we come closer to satisfying our customer, accomplishing our mission, and avoiding the economic decline many large companies are experiencing today.

You will work in teams of four now, to define specific behaviors that demonstrate standards like quality and respect. To illustrate, if hostesses in a restaurant are required to be customer-oriented, that might mean:

✓ *Smiling at customers.*
✓ *Learning and using their names if they are repeat customers.*

97

✓ *Addressing them as "sir" or "miss" or "ma'm" if they are not repeat customers.*

✓ *Being honest about how long they will have to wait for a table.*

✓ *Remembering to ask if they prefer smoking or nonsmoking.*

And so on. It is important that general phrases—such as "be customer-oriented"—have specifics attached to them.

STEPS TO FOLLOW (CONTINUED)
2. Form teams of four or five, preferably with people from the same department or same organization.

3. Distribute Handout 37-1 and allow about 10 minutes for completion.

4. Call on each team to briefly share its insights.

DISCUSSION QUESTIONS
✓ How can we verify our assumptions about customers' expectations?

✓ Who are your internal customers?

✓ How and how often are their opinions solicited?

✓ What individuals should serve on a cross-functional team to improve some aspect of customer relations?

GAME STRETCHER
Ask for a volunteer to collect and compile the responses and then to share them with the company's customer service department. If there is no such department, ask the volunteer to write a short article for the company newsletter based on the ideas presented.

HOW-TO'S FOR THE WHAT-TO-DO'S

1. In your small group, list the names of three internal or external customers for your department or your organization.

   a. _____

   b. _____

   c. _____

2. Tell what you think is the most important expectation each customer has. What does he or she expect us to do? (In the future, your department or organization should verify these assumptions.)

   a. _____

   b. _____

   c. _____

3. Now select just one item from your answers to question 2. This selection represents what the customer expects you to do. The next step is to list below six how-to's. Specify what the expectation means and what it does not mean. Try to come up with three verb phrases for each column.

The customer expects us to _____.

In order to meet that expectation, we:

Must	Must not
a. _____	**a.** _____
b. _____	**b.** _____
c. _____	**c.** _____

38

YOU CAN QUOTE ME ON THAT!

OBJECTIVE   To expose participants to the thoughts of noted authorities in the **customer service** field

TIME   Approximately 10 minutes

MATERIALS   Handout 38-1: Who said that?, one for each participant; inexpensive prize for the winner

MINILECTURE   *We all need to be reminded from time to time of the big picture, of issues that are sometimes forgotten in the busyness of business. We need to think about Joe L. Griffith's assertion that "the customer is our employer." Today I'm going to share with you some thoughts about customer service, spoken by famous individuals who are used to working with and thinking about the customer. The prize goes to the first person who can correctly match at least five individuals with the ideas they expressed about the way to treat the users of our products and/or services.*

ANSWERS   1. D; 2. I; 3. F; 4. E; 5. H; 6. A; 7. B; 8. C; 9. G

STEPS TO FOLLOW
1. Distribute Handout 38-1.
2. Allow about 10 minutes for completion.
3. Call on those who feel they have the right answers until someone wins the prize.

DISCUSSION QUESTIONS
✓ What pithy, memorable statement could you create about the way customers should be treated?
✓ How well do you know your customer?
✓ What are the causes of poor customer treatment?
✓ What prevents some customers from complaining?

GAME STRETCHER   Have a volunteer begin a collection of customer service quotations. Post them periodically on a bulletin board or E-mail.

WHO SAID THAT?

Directions: Match the famous persons with the not quite as famous statements they made about treating customers. When you finish, raise your hand and claim your prize (assuming you are both first and correct).

A. "When a customer enters my store, forget me. He is king."

B. "My audience is $3.95 readers."

C. "Undertake not what you cannot perform but be careful to keep your promise."

D. "The most important yardstick of your success will be how you treat other people."

E. "Can you explain, in 25 words or less, what is absolutely special about [your product/service], what will make people say ≡ 'Holy moly!'"

F. "The customer is always right."

G. "Consumer research takes the pulse of the consumer's reactions and demands, and seeks explanations for the findings."

H. "If you don't genuinely like your customers, the chances are they won't buy."

I. "There is only one boss. The customer."

1. Barbara Bush

2. Sam Walton

3. Anonymous

4. Tom Peters

5. Thomas J. Watson, Jr.

6. John Wanamaker

7. John MacDonald

8. George Washington

9. Dr. W. Edwards Deming

39

CUSTOMERS' DREAM TEAM

OBJECTIVE
To identify, from the customer's perspective, the public figures who are **getting close to the customer** and who are serving as customer advocates

TIME
Approximately 15 minutes

MATERIALS
Chart paper; marking pens; masking tape

MINILECTURE
"Get the confidence of the public, and you will have no difficulty getting their patronage," H. George Selfridge tells us. *"Remember always that the recollection of quality remains long after price is forgotten."*

One way or another, customers get satisfaction. If it is not from improved service/products from us, then it is by seeking another company to do business with. Sometimes, customers will even seek an advocate such as Ralph Nader or the Better Business Bureau, with whom they can file a formal complaint.

What public figures do you think have the fullest understanding of the customer? Who truly understands and reflects the importance of customer needs as they produce goods or services? With your team, create a Customers' Dream Team—seven Americans, living or dead, who you believe are or were close to the heart of the customer. One recommendation: You should not have all white males on that team. Let the team makeup reflect the nation's makeup.

STEPS TO FOLLOW
1. Divide the class into small groups of four or five. Distribute chart paper and marking pens.
2. Allow about 10 minutes for them to name their teams—a minimum of seven players.
3. Post the Dream Team lists and compare. Call on a few participants from each team at random, and ask for the rationale behind their selection of a given Dream Team member.

DISCUSSION QUESTIONS
✓ Why did you select the individuals you did?
✓ What traits do they have in common?
✓ How could we make our customers more aware of the individuals in our company who possess the same traits or concern for the customer?

GAME STRETCHER
(10-20 minutes) Participants could devise Dream Teams for any other aspect of their business life. For example, who would serve on the Manufacturing Dream Team, the Medical Dream Team, etc. They could set their own boundaries with respect to a period of time, the type of contribution, and so on.

OVERVIEW: DETERMINING WHAT THE CUSTOMER EXPECTS

Pre-TQM, the voice of the customer was heard only when it was raised in complaint about the quality of a product or service. The problem with listening to angry voices is that we assume the contented customers are totally satisfied with the quality they are receiving. In truth, many dissatisfied customers do not take the time to complain; they simply take their business elsewhere. (Network executives, to illustrate, know that every one phone call of complaint about programming represents several thousand other concerned viewers.)

To believe that no complaints equal no dissatisfaction is to run the risk of customers silently switching their allegiance to another provider. Today, the voice of the customer is not only listened to, it is invited to be heard at the inception stage of new products.

Believing that customers define quality, organizations actively solicit input from them in the design stage. As products and services are being planned, customers are asked to answer tough questions about the company and its outputs:

What are we doing well?

What are we not doing well?

What are we doing that we should not be doing?

What are we not doing that we should be doing?

What constitutes value for you?

What do typical customers want, need, deserve, expect, require?

What, specifically, are we doing to respond to what they want, need, deserve, expect, require?

What would delight our customers?

The quality-conscious organization seeks answers to such questions not only from customers but from every department and work unit. Quality advocates within such organizations take input and translate it to every relevant function. This quality function deployment, as it is known, ensures that what is important to the customer is shared with appropriate departments as the importance message travels from the design stage through production.

40

THE LEADERSHIP VACUUM

OBJECTIVE   To illustrate that when **customers' expectations** are not met, customers often take action

TIME   Approximately 10 minutes

MATERIALS   None

MINILECTURE   Note: Because of the nature of this game, the minilecture follows the description of the method and focuses on the Discussion Questions.

METHOD   Standing in front of the room, read or write or assemble papers or chat with another person for as long as it takes before someone in the class exerts leadership to fill the vacuum deliberately created by you. Even if it takes 15 minutes, wait until someone in the class finally says something. Typically, a participant clears his or her throat and then diplomatically (or not) asks, "Excuse me, but do you think we could get started with the class?" This, of course, is your clue to begin the lecture. [*Note:* Do not wait more than 15 minutes for leadership to emerge. If no one acts assertively, explain what you were doing (deliberately awaiting a customer complaint) and then begin the discussion.]

DISCUSSION QUESTIONS
- ✓ What expectations do you have for a training session?
- ✓ What expectations do you have for the suppliers who give you what you need to do your work?
- ✓ What expectations do your customers have for the work that you supply them?
- ✓ Do your customers articulate their needs to you?
- ✓ Do you articulate your needs to your suppliers?
- ✓ What is your response to John Erskine's comment that "a leader is one who knows where he wants to go, then gets up and goes"?
- ✓ How can customer/supplier communications be improved?

41

MUTUAL UNDERSTANDING

OBJECTIVE

To illustrate the gap between the customer's understanding of the output and the process owner's knowledge of output in order to improve understanding of **customers'** and **suppliers' needs**

TIME

Approximately 20 minutes

MATERIALS

Two small shopping bags, each filled with six to ten small, everyday, completely different food/household products (gum, soup, jello, deodorant, ointment, vitamins, etc.); optional token prizes for the winning team

MINILECTURE

Total Quality is often defined as meeting customers' needs and reasonable expectations. Sometimes customers' expectations are unreasonable—usually because they are unaware of the constraints and conditions under which process owners perform their work.

To illustrate the gap between what the customer sees as the output or end product and what the process owner knows about how the output was created, I'm going to ask you to work in two teams.

STEPS TO FOLLOW

1. Divide the class into two large groups. Separate them as much as possible so that the two teams cannot see or hear what the other is doing. Give each team a product-filled shopping bag.

2. Working together quietly, each team selects at least three of the items in the bag and records the ingredients for each.

3. They then exchange their lists. The winning team is the one that can correctly identify the most items using the ingredients list only.

DISCUSSION QUESTIONS

✓ Of what aspects of your work is your customer unaware?

✓ How can an organization develop appreciation of the work being done?

42

REDUCING CUSTOMER FRUSTRATION

OBJECTIVE
To have participants consider what causes frustration for customers and what can increase **customer satisfaction**

TIME
Approximately 10 minutes

MATERIALS
Handout 42-1: The Laws of the (Customer) Land; optional token prizes for one team

MINILECTURE
"The Law of the Supermarket," some anonymous shopper has remarked, is that, *"the other line moves faster."* Researchers have found, though, that customers do not object as much to waiting if they feel they are being treated fairly. What might constitute fairness in the mind of a customer? [Have a brief discussion. Some ideas that might exemplify fairness include these: being served in turn, having customer servers show sensitivity to the long wait, having customer servers who do not prolong the wait by engaging other customers in idle chatter.]
    Work in small teams now to consider what frustrates various customers and also what lighthearted laws can reflect that frustration.

STEPS TO FOLLOW
1. Divide the class into small groups and distribute the handout.

2. Award prizes to the first team to create three laws.

DISCUSSION QUESTIONS
✓ What recent frustrating experiences have you had as a customer?

✓ How could your frustration have been lessened?

✓ Who are your internal customers (i.e., who receives the outputs of your work)? What might be causing frustration for them?

✓ How could you ascertain whether your suspicions are correct?

✓ In what ways do the various establishments you frequent (restaurants, universities, grocery stores, doctors offices) attempt to learn what may be frustrating you?

✓ If they are not making any attempt to learn, what might a proactive customer do?

THE LAWS OF THE (CUSTOMER) LAND

Directions: As quickly as you can, devise a tongue in cheek law for at least three of the following locations in which customers (internal and external) conduct business.

A. Mail room   Law: _____

B. Copy room   Law: _____

C. Meeting room   Law: _____

D. Emergency ward   Law: _____

E. Dentist's office   Law: _____

F. Motor Vehicles Department   Law: _____

G. Bank   Law: _____

H. Library   Law: _____

I. Car repair shop   Law: _____

J. Other: _____   Law: _____

If time permits, brainstorm some ways that frustration might be reduced for customers who conduct business in these places.

_____

_____

_____

_____

_____

_____

_____

_____

_____

_____

_____

_____

43

FRONTWARDS AND BACKWARDS

OBJECTIVE   To encourage greater attention to **customer needs**

TIME   Approximately 10 minutes

MATERIALS   Transparency 43-1: Historical Utterances

MINILECTURE   *There is an old Spanish saying: "To become a great bullfighter, one must learn how the bull thinks." That adage can be applied to customer relations. If we are to truly serve our customers, we must get close to them. We must hear not only what they are saying, but also what they are not saying. In addition, we need to see things as they see things. We must look at the products and services we offer from many different angles: What is clear in hindsight is not always so obvious initially.*

METHOD   Divide the class into pairs and show Transparency 43-1. Ask if anyone notices something unusual about the sentences. (*Note:* Ask if anyone has already seen these sentences or others like them. If so, ask that individual not to participate in the game; he or she can serve as a general observer instead.) Segue into a discussion of the need to examine situations from several different points of view.

DISCUSSION QUESTIONS   ✓ What causes the filters that prevent us from truly understanding our customers?

✓ What can the organization do to encourage thinking that goes outside the box beyond the obvious?

✓ Does your organization have focus groups, teams of customers that advise on operations from the customer's point of view? If so, what good advice have they shared? If not, could focus groups be assembled?

✓ Have you ever, pretending to be a potential customer, called your own switchboard to see how callers are treated?

GAME STRETCHER   (10–15 minutes) Sentences (like those on the transparency) that read frontwards and backwards the same way are called *palindromes*. Encourage participants to create some that pertain to customers.

HISTORICAL UTTERANCES?

"Able was I 'ere I saw Elba."—Napoleon

"Madam, I'm Adam."—Adam in Garden of Eden

"A man, a plan, a canal—Panama!"—Teddy Roosevelt

SECTION 6

ROLES QUALITY ADVOCATES PLAY

Quality does not just happen. It is created by an ongoing series of strategies that include developing a mission, determining what responsibility each employee has in the execution of that mission, and enabling/empowering employees to carry out their responsibilities.

This section delineates some of the roles people in Quality organizations play. For each role, at least one skill building game is provided to develop understanding of what the roles require. Too often, organizations plunge into the middle of team projects without first defining the expectations for members of the team. Exercises like these help to clarify expectations.

OVERVIEW: CHAMPION

Teams find many talents and resources among their members. However, they also find that, by going outside the circle of team membership, they can locate other talents and resources. Teams that have identified a member of upper management to be their champion soon learn that this external advocate has a clout beyond the scope of their own efforts.

External advocates, for example, work to build a critical mass of converts at all levels of the organization but especially among their peers. Such a climate of receptivity lessens the time and effort required by teams to gain acceptance of their ideas. The champion is also instrumental in providing appropriate training for all levels of the organization. Again, the more widely accepted the tenets of Quality, the more readily teams can advanced their improvement causes.

Champions are exemplars whose actions bespeak a commitment to Quality. Their stand is not a tentative one: It is clear to others that they understand both Quality in terms of the philosophy and quality in terms of the excellence of the product being manufactured or the service being delivered. Beyond understanding, champions help others understand the importance of the direction in which the organization is moving along its path to Quality.

They are also proponents of statistical thinking and of decisions based on facts rather than on emotions or opinions. Such thinking, ideally, is evinced by all members of the organization in varying degrees of sophistication. Champions also build partnerships inside and outside the organization, doing all they can to solidify the foundation of Quality on which decisions ultimately rest.

44

SETTING DIRECTION

OBJECTIVE

To provide insight into the **role of the team champion**

TIME

Approximately 10 minutes

MATERIALS

None

MINILECTURE

Phyllis Bottome notes, "There are two ways of meeting difficulties. You alter the difficulties or you alter yourself to meet them." For team members, though, there is a third choice: finding a champion to serve as advocate for the team and its purpose.

To illustrate the dual role of the champion as repository of the organization's history and supporter of efforts to continuously improve, let me share a puzzle with you:

> *Assume you are attending a Quality conference in Rochester, New York. You and a handful of your classmates have decided to take a long hike from your hotel in downtown Rochester to the nearby suburb of Chili. Soon, though, you find you are lost. Finally, you come upon a signpost, but it has been knocked down by the wind. It says (with appropriate pointing arrows): Rochester: 10; Chili: 2; Fairport: 8; Perinton: 22; Pittsford: 18. How can you find your way to Chili?*

STEPS TO FOLLOW

1. Allow a few moments for someone to figure out the answer (or supply it if no one does): Since they know the direction from which they came, they can place the signpost back in the earth with the arrow for Rochester pointing in the direction they have been coming from. This will enable them to know in what direction they must travel in order to reach Chili.

2. Draw parallels from the puzzle to the role of the team champion, who:

Typically has a sense of organizational history.

Is close enough to senior management to have a sense of future direction.

Can serve as a guide.

Can prevent the team from getting lost in bureaucratic mazes.

Can help restore the direction or focus of the team.

✓ Who in your organization would make a good team champion?

✓ In which team activities would you involve the champion?

✓ What would you ask or expect of your champion?

✓ What would he or she expect of your team?

GAME STRETCHER

(15-20 minutes) Have participants draft a letter inviting someone in upper management to serve as their team champion. The letter should clearly outline what responsibilities the champion is expected to assume.

OVERVIEW: MANAGER

Managers in Quality organizations play a pivotal role because teams need assistance in:

✓ Finding the time away from work requirements to hold regular meetings.

✓ Finding a place to meet.

✓ Obtaining resources.

✓ Learning new tools for doing Quality.

✓ Gathering data and then in reporting those data to the Quality Council.

Managers are not typically part of the teams whose members they supervise, although they may be invited to sit in on meetings occasionally.

Once managers have developed their personal understanding of Quality and their own definition of quality, they share them with department members. They are wise enough not to expect quick fixes from their teams, knowing that teams must undergo their own transformations. (Bruce Tuckman's depiction of the team cycle—Form, Storm, Norm, Perform—is a cycle that requires time.)

Managers who support the idea of continuous improvement recognize that improvement necessitates change. They enable others to adapt to the changes that inevitably accompany transformations. Above all, they recognize the inevitability of changes in their own role.

The concept of leader as servant is initially difficult for many managers to accept. But, if Dr. Juran is correct (as we believe he is) in asserting that "quality will be accomplished project by project and in no other way," then quality managers must support and serve the teams that work on projects.

The concept of the manager as an authoritarian figure is fast disappearing. (Most employees would wish it a speedy departure.) In its stead emerges the concept of the manager as a facilitator—a facilitator not necessarily as encourager of team processes, but as enabler of improvement undertakings.

45

MANAGERIAL MATCHES

OBJECTIVE   To develop awareness of the **manager's role in allocating necessary resources for the team**

TIME   Approximately 10 minutes

MATERIALS   Nine matchsticks for each small group of six or seven

MINILECTURE   *Shifting paradigms is not easy. We've learned to view the world in a certain way and refocusing our gaze requires new learning. "If you see in any given situation only what everybody else can see, you can be said to be so much a representative of your culture that you are a victim of it." The words of S. I. Hayakawa encourage us to think in new ways. Let's try thinking in nontypical ways. Here are nine matchsticks. Can you create four triangles with them?* [Note: After a few minutes, share the solution with them.]

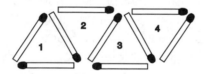

STEPS TO FOLLOW

1. Divide the class into small groups and distribute the matchsticks.

2. Allow about 5 minutes for them to solve the problem.

3. Complete the minilecture as follows:

In these tough economic times, we are all being asked to do more with less. Our first reaction is often one of despair. Yet, with motivation and creativity, we can often find a way to do more with less. It's often a question of using our innate talents. For example, it is possible to create four triangles using only six matchsticks. Can you do it in the next 3 minutes? [Note: The solution is a three-dimensional one.]

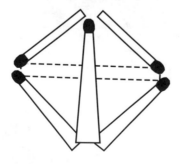

We often need assistance from managers, assistance that takes the form of released time for team meetings, resources, or data collection help. We depend on managers' ability to meet production goals even though department members are not at work, but instead are working on team projects.

DISCUSSION QUESTIONS

✓ Dr. Juran speaks of increasing the "vital few" aspects of our work and minimizing the "trivial many." If we are able to do this, we will probably increase our output and actually do more with less. What are the "vital few" aspects of your work?

✓ Can you think of examples in which Yankee ingenuity was used to solve organizational problems?

✓ How can we develop the ability to think outside the box?

GAME STRETCHER

(10 minutes) A favorite interview technique is to have a team of applicants work for 5 minutes to devise as long a list as possible of ways to improve a bathtub. The second half of the assignment asks them to work for only 4 minutes to create a similar list (with no duplicated ideas) and to work with one less person on their team. Use this technique to illustrate doing more with less.

OVERVIEW: TEAM LEADER

Team leaders participate on occasion as regular members of the team. Most of the time, however, the team leaders function as captains of the team and are charged with ensuring that their teams reach their destinations. The leaders set the agenda, assign tasks, and serve as liaison with management. While they share equally in the successes or failures of the team, the leaders shoulder the additional responsibility of being in charge.

Team leaders set the direction for the team—members with their input and acceptance, of course. They keep the ultimate outcome uppermost in the minds of all team members. We expect team leaders to possess the necessary task and maintenance skills, but we also expect them to have the necessary tools for running effective meetings; the tools for gathering, analyzing, and reporting data; and the tools for making persuasive presentations to the Quality Council.

Additionally, team leaders, by virtue of their role, are expected to interface with various other individuals and departments and sometimes to go beyond the physical confines of the office or plant to find support in the larger community. Being a team leader requires outstanding communication skills as well as meeting and people skills.

46

COMMON CENTS

OBJECTIVE   To develop **divergent thinking** needed for **problem solving**

TIME   Approximately 10 minutes

MATERIALS   Transparency 46-1

MINILECTURE   *"The task of the leader," Henry Kissinger asserts, "is to get his people from where they are to where they have not been." One way the leader does this is to encourage thinking that causes us to view situations from a divergent viewpoint. See if you can figure out the answer to this question and then we'll talk further about this kind of thinking. [Show transparency.]*

STEPS TO FOLLOW

1. Show the transparency and give participants about 5 minutes to figure out the answer: Because 1973 pennies are almost 2000 pennies and so are worth almost twenty dollars."

2. Lead a discussion focusing on the need to look at problems from multiple perspectives and the need to hear differing points of view.

DISCUSSION QUESTIONS

✓ What mindset forced our thinking into a set pattern?

✓ How can team leaders encourage divergent thinking as teams tackle the improvement of work processes?

✓ We often put on blinders that prevent us from looking at problems in fresh, original ways. What are some solutions that did not come readily (or at all) to you or to your team because you were looking at a problem in a typical, traditional way?

✓ Often a given word or visual clue (1973 as opposed to 1,973) hooks our thinking and does not release it easily. We remain set in a mode and are not able to explore new directions. What is your problem-solving approach? Your team's?

Why are
1973 pennies
worth almost
twenty dollars?

47

SOMETHING'S FISHY HERE

OBJECTIVE   To illustrate the importance of **vision in leadership**

TIME   Approximately 10 minutes

MATERIALS   Transparency 47-1; flip chart; marking pen

MINILECTURE   *"Anything you do is everything you do" is wisdom offered in a Buddhist saying. In other words, we find contained in the smallest act the same values that are reflected in all acts. It is especially important for team leaders to reflect, in all they do, their faith that the team will ultimately meet its goal. Leaders may not be certain how the team will do that, but they are always certain of the final result.*

Leaders envision the final output and then work backwards to plan the path leading to the output. Look at this transparency now [show transparency] and believe me when I tell you that it can be drawn in one continuous line. Assume you are a team leader, confident that this can be done. All you have to do now is figure out how. [Note: The following figure shows how a single line can lead to the complete drawing.]

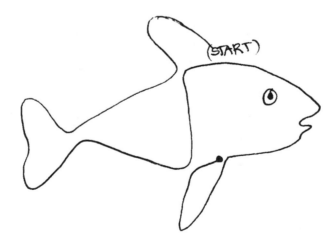

STEPS TO FOLLOW   **1.** Divide the class into groups of two or three.

2. After showing the transparency, allow about 5 minutes for them to figure out the solution. If no one does, demonstrate the figure above on the flip chart.

DISCUSSION QUESTIONS

✓ What is the vision statement for your organization?

✓ How has it been communicated to the workforce?

✓ What forces impacted its creation?

✓ What strategic plans have been articulated for reaching the ultimate vision?

✓ What is the difference between a vision statement and a mission statement?

✓ On what bases are team leaders selected in your organization?

GAME STRETCHER

(10 minutes) Have participants prepare a vision statement for the training session. If time permits, they can also prepare a mission statement and even a values statement.

OVERVIEW: FACILITATOR

The role of facilitator is so important that it requires special training. Many of us have had opportunities to demonstrate our leadership over the years, thus the transition to team leadership should not be especially difficult. But few of us have been asked to facilitate, and so people often enter this role lacking clarity about the difference between the leader's role and the facilitator's role. Before we point out the difference, note that a team can be successful with a weak leader and a strong facilitator or vice versa. But it cannot succeed if both the leader and the facilitator are lacking skills.

Leaders are charged with the task. They do everything necessary to see that goals are met. Sometimes, though, leaders are so focused on the task that they overlook the other components that constitute effective teams and effective team meetings. Only if the other components are not being attended to should facilitators step in and assist. Otherwise, facilitators run the risk of dominating the meeting. Nonstop leadership simply does not fall within the facilitators' role or responsibilities.

In short, facilitators make the meeting "facile" in the most literal sense of the word. When things start to get difficult, facilitators step in to attend to members' physical, emotional, and psychological well-being. They also have some responsibility to attend to the project's well-being: If consensus needs to be reached, if recording needs to be done, if a summary is called for, if members need to be reminded of past successes—all these and more fall within the scope of the facilitators' job.

48

VERBAL FACILITY

OBJECTIVE

To advance understanding of the **facilitator's responsibility for encouraging dispirited teams**

TIME

Approximately 15 minutes

MATERIALS

Transparency 48-1

MINILECTURE

Simple words are often the best. They are memorable, inspirational, and able to rally a group to move forward rather than remain mired in negativity or stuck at an impasse.

STEPS TO FOLLOW

1. Divide the class into teams of three and show Transparency 48-1. Point out that some of the most inspirational thoughts are very simple statements:

"Drive out fear" from Dr. Deming.

"Eliminate turf wars" from Dr. Juran.

Or from Winston Churchill: "Never give up."

Allow about 10 minutes for teams to devise two or three sayings that facilitators could use to encourage a dispirited team.

2. Have the teams share their thoughts; post them if possible.

DISCUSSION QUESTIONS

✓ What makes a statement quotable?

✓ In what other ways can a facilitator encourage a team?

✓ What are some words that have been a turning point in your life during a time when you were dispirited?

GAME STRETCHER

(10 minutes) Have participants discuss ways their sayings could be made more visible in the organization.

This, too, shall pass.

Live and let live.

In God we trust.

49

GETTING YOUR DOLLAR'S WORTH

OBJECTIVE   To emphasize the importance of allocating **team meeting time**

TIME   Approximately 25 minutes

MATERIALS   Flip charts (ideally one for each team); marking pens

MINILECTURE   *Millionaire Malcolm Forbes once remarked that, "There is never enough time, unless you're serving it." Facilitators often play the role of time monitors, reminding the team that time is a limited resource, one that must be used wisely and well. The facilitator will use the following diagram [draw picture of a dollar bill on the flip chart] to decide how time will be spent during the 20-minute meeting.*

We'll get some practice with this today as you engage in a team assignment that will take about 20 minutes: Brainstorm a list of 15 to 20 ways in which an organization can develop awareness of TQM, and then prioritize the team's top three choices. Before the team leader begins conducting the meeting, the facilitator will help you decide how your dollar's worth of time (representing 20 minutes) will be spent on the assignment. This graphic [point to flip chart drawing] will be your unofficial agenda.

STEPS TO FOLLOW

1. Divide the class into teams of eight or nine, and appoint a leader and a facilitator for each team.

2. Have the facilitator work with the team for about 5 minutes to develop the dollar's worth of time agenda.

3. After meeting for 20 minutes, each team appoints a spokesperson to share the top three ideas from the brainstormed list.

DISCUSSION QUESTIONS

✓ What causes time to be wasted in meetings?

✓ When should the facilitator step in to keep the meeting on track?

✓ Does every meeting need an agenda—formal or not? Explain.

OVERVIEW: EMPLOYEES

Employees in a Quality organization work on teams. In so doing, they demonstrate their belief in the Quality philosophy and their belief in the synergy released by collective effort.

But employees in a Quality organization can demonstrate their adherence to Quality in other ways as well. When they offer suggestions, when they benchmark, when they take classes, and when they teach classes, they are demonstrating their faith in the power of TQM to transform organizations. When they spread the Quality word, when they write articles or give presentations about their organization's Quality experience, when they celebrate National Quality Month (in October)—working individually or in teams in all these ways—employees illustrate that theirs is indeed a Quality organization.

In organizations driven by Quality principles, all employees work on teams. In the beginning of the Quality conversion, however, team members may have to be appointed (better still, invited to serve). In time, though, when Quality fever overtakes an organization, employees volunteer to serve on teams, they suggest ideas for projects, and they offer ideas for process improvement and for meeting improvement. They work actively to improve their individual meeting skills, as well as the meeting skills of the team as a whole. They come into their own and in so doing display heightened initiative and inventiveness.

50

TEAMWORK

OBJECTIVE	To develop understanding of how **cross-functional teams** operate
TIME	Approximately 5 minutes
MATERIALS	Transparency 50-1; dollar bill(s) for demonstration; box of paper clips
MINILECTURE	*United teams can have outstanding achievement. Those that are fractional fail themselves, the project, and the organization. No matter what the problem, teamwork can help solve it. As John Peer observes, "When working toward the solution of a problem, it always helps if you know the answer." The human resource answer to the problems facing teams is always teamwork. The other solution results from that teamwork.*
	Perhaps we can best understand how people from several different departments within an organization can work together by considering the team composed of representatives from different departments. The cross-functional team members represent their various functions, but in time they form new allegiances to the team itself. Let's see how this works. Would each of you take out a dollar bill? A five or ten will do just as well if you don't have a dollar bill.

STEPS TO FOLLOW

1. Distribute two paper clips to each participant.
2. Show Transparency 50-1 as you instruct them to fold a dollar bill and to clip it in two places, as shown in the diagram.
3. Next they are to hold both ends of the dollar bill and pull. An amazing thing happens: The clips unite. Draw parallels to the union of team members who come from different parts of the organization to serve on a cross-functional team.

DISCUSSION QUESTION

✓ What problem in your organization could be solved by such teams?

51

QUALITY AT THE ATOMIC LEVEL

OBJECTIVE   To build awareness of **synergy,** the powerful effect of individual contributions to the team effort

TIME   Approximately 5 minutes

MATERIALS   Transparency 51-1

MINILECTURE   *A. Bartlett Giammatti, in his role as baseball commissioner, wisely observed, that "No one man is superior to the game." While individual contributions are individually valuable, and, it is hoped, valued, the combined contributions yield a power unlikely to be achieved except by cohesion. To illustrate this, I'd like you to look at this transparency with me* [show it now], *and see how products of increasing complexity and sophistication are developed one element at a time. The remarkable result of teamed effort is termed* synergy.

METHOD   Show Transparency 51-1 one line at a time, starting with "STARTLING" as the final collective output. Before revealing the next line, ask if anyone can think of a new word that could be created merely by removing one letter. Do the same with each of the lines. The letters that would be removed each time are T, L, A, R, T, G, S, and N.

DISCUSSION QUESTIONS
✓ To what extent do your feel your contributions are valued in the organization?

✓ When is the last time a manager asked you what is the greatest contribution you can make to the organization?

✓ When is the last time you mentioned this contribution without being asked?

✓ What can the (team) leader do to encourage full participation in the organizational efforts?

GAME STRETCHER   (5–10 minutes) See if participants can find other words that can be reduced to their atomic level.

STARTLING
STARLING
STARING
STRING
STING
SING
SIN
IN
I

SECTION 7
THE POWER OF TEAMWORK

What distinguishes people in a team from people in a group is their sense of commitment. Because a common goal unites their efforts, team members can move toward the same foreseeable outcome envisioned by those others whose cooperative efforts are tied to the same vision.

The purpose of this section is to trace the sequence of steps in which teams typically engage:

1. The selection of a project

2. The collection of data relevant to the process they wish to improve, the problem they wish to solve, or the project they wish to undertake

3. The presentation of their findings to the Quality Council (at various milestone stages)

4. The celebration of their successes

Two games are presented to sharpen the skills required by participants at each stage.

OVERVIEW: SELECTING THE PROJECT

In its larger sense, the *project* is the work the team has undertaken, and the project most often undertaken is a process to be improved. Teams gather baseline data to determine if there is a need for improvement. If so, they seek permission from the Quality Council to proceed. Upon obtaining approval, they devise the improvement plan and check to see whether it does indeed improve the process. If so, they act—with further approval of the Council—to implement their improvement. If not, they make changes in the original plan, or perhaps abandon it altogether to start all over again with a new plan.

As teams undertake this process, they exemplify Dr. Walter Shewhart's idea of the PDCA cycle—Plan, Do, Check, Act.

On occasion a team undertakes a project in the narrower sense, such as starting a Quality library or sponsoring a Quality Forum. They may also tackle solving a problem unrelated to processes. One example might be sexism in the workplace, low morale, etc.

The processes, projects, and problems are typically defined by the Quality Council and assigned to teams, although some teams can take a project to the Council and ask for permission to proceed with it. Membership on teams is typically defined by the Quality Council as well—especially in a military organization. It is also possible for employees to *ask* to serve on a team when they feel they can make a valuable contribution. Employees can form their own team as well.

The Quality movement has created an attitude revolution. Corporate citizens are reassessing their fidelity to missions, to management, and to themselves. Those who have made the pledge to teamwork have simultaneously pledged to make data-based decisions. Underlying the intentions of teams is the understanding that baseline data must be gathered before the intervention has begun. As the project is underway, additional data are gathered so that teams (and ultimately the approval-granting Quality Council) can compare the results of the project with the preproject standings.

52

IT'S A QUESTION OF QUESTIONS

OBJECTIVE

To have participants consider questions that should be raised at the first **team meeting**

TIME

Approximately 15 minutes

MATERIALS

Transparency 52-1

MINILECTURE

It doesn't matter whether a team has assembled to select its own project or the project has been assigned to them. Certain questions should be raised and addressed at the first team meeting. The leader should elicit the questions that members inevitably bring to the first meeting and should assure the members that there are no silly questions. Alfred North Whitehead's statement [show transparency now] should help bring out those questions. The leader should plan to address other questions as well.

You will work in teams now to consider the questions that should be asked and answered at the first team meeting. Here are a few to get you started:

✓ *Does the project help the organization carry out its overall mission?*

✓ *What will be expected of us?*

✓ *What new knowledge will I have to acquire?*

METHOD

Divide the class into three large teams. Assign each team the task of coming up with 10 questions. Team 1 will ask (and ideally answer in general terms) questions related to the organization. Team 2 will list questions that team members would have in relation to their work as a team. Team 3 will list questions related to individual concerns. [*Note:* Encourage atypical questions. One team, for example, raised these oxymoronic questions: "What is the reward for failure?" "What is the penalty for success?" Upon scrutiny, these questions have merit.]

DISCUSSION QUESTIONS

✓ What would the first meeting agenda look like?

✓ How can the team leader ensure that all questions are asked?

✓ What can be done to ensure the team's project is an appropriate one?

✓ What body language indications of questions should the leader be alert to?

"The 'silly question' is the first intimation of some totally new development."

—A. N. Whitehead

53

TEAM VALUES

OBJECTIVE   To encourage analysis of the team project in terms of **personal and organizational values**

TIME   Approximately 15 minutes

MATERIALS   None

MINILECTURE   *Most of us have not taken the time to itemize what we value in life. Some of our values we hold within ourselves. We do not need to articulate them. Others, though, we may say we hold when in fact there is little evidence we do. Or we may not even realize we have a certain value until confronted with evidence that suggests we do. One good way to see if your lifestyle reflects the things you value is to look at your checkbook. Would you take a moment to get out your checkbook?* [Pause] *Hold it close now so that no one else can see what you are looking at. As you scan the last several months, what things are you spending money on? Are you putting your money where your values are?*

STEPS TO FOLLOW

1. After participants have had a chance to jot down the values reflected by their checkbook and to share their insights—if they wish to—with a partner, have them work together to determine what values their organizations have or should have and what values their current (or past) team has or should have.

2. Call on each pair to tell how one value is reflected in the choice of a project that teams typically pursue. (For example, seeking to improve a process indicates the values of efficiency, continuous improvement and/or reducing waste. If the project were to hold a conference, the inherent values might be sharing and knowledge.)

DISCUSSION QUESTIONS

✓ Do you agree with the assertion that expenditures reflect values?

✓ What visible evidence is there in your own organization that stated values are used as operating guidelines?

✓ What do we value as a society?

✓ Should values be taught in the schools? If so, which ones?

OVERVIEW: MAKING DATA-BASED DECISIONS

We will never have all the facts we could use to operate at peak efficiency. But we usually have enough to make reasonably effective decisions. If you view decision making on a continuum, you recognize the type of decision maker at one end who is a freewheeler—making decisions with intuition rather than data, operating at gut level rather than the investigative level. At the other end is the individual who suffers paralysis by analysis—the person who cannot make the decision without gathering more data.

Decision making is seldom easy, but most decisions can be modified at a later time if the initial direction appears to be wrong. In the world of Quality, data are gathered and decisions are based on them. Making decisions instinctively may work for highly experienced executives and well trained psychologists, but for teams data-based decisions work best.

In the world of Quality, one maxim influences the work of all teams, "Without backup data, you are just another person with an opinion." The insistence on data is the responsibility of the managers and leaders whose actions impact the work of the team. The team leader especially is charged with explaining the need for data-based decision making, ensuring that the members have the necessary training and tools, and sustaining the team as they gather, interpret, and then report their findings.

The ultimate goal of all process improvement teams is the reduction of the variation associated with the operation of the process. A related but less important goal of the team is to reduce the variation in how the team operates. As teams work to stabilize work processes, their relationships ideally gel and so the team process is stabilized as well.

Disparate and often extraneous factors appear at early team meetings. Similarly, unexamined processes usually contain redundancies and inefficiencies that flowcharts can identify and help eliminate. As teams become more aligned in their thinking about process improvement, the process itself becomes more aligned in the steps required to produce a high-quality output.

54

A NUMBER OF NUMBERS

OBJECTIVE

To show, in a lighthearted way, that **data need proper interpretation/expression**

TIME

Approximately 5 minutes

MATERIALS

Four small prizes

MINILECTURE

Simeon Strunsky has defined statistics as "the heart of democracy." If we are serving on quality teams, our organizations must believe—to some extent—in the participative style of management, a style that is democratic by its very nature. We must take care, though, in interpreting and then sharing the statistics we have collected. Let me show you what I mean. I am going to read some numbers aloud. There will be a small prize for the first person to write down the number I speak and then hold it up for us to see.

STEPS TO FOLLOW

1. Speak the following numbers and award a prize each time to the first person who holds up the appropriate number:

Two thousand four hundred and six dollars ($2406)

Five thousand five hundred and forty-nine dollars ($5549)

Seven thousand seven hundred and seventy-seven dollars ($7777)

Eleven thousand eleven hundred and eleven dollars ($11,111)

2. Ask why it took longer for the class to get the final number correct.

DISCUSSION QUESTIONS

✓ What is your interpretation of Strunsky's definition?

✓ Can you think of a time in your organization's history when numbers were expressed incorrectly with serious consequences?

✓ What charts do teams typically use to transform raw data?

GAME STRETCHER

(10 minutes) Have participants think about other statistics they may have committed to memory—about history, Internet, education, economics, societal problems. How can those statistics be presented to others in a meaningful way?

55

FROM SURVEY TO CHART

OBJECTIVE	To provide practice in converting raw data to a **bar chart**
TIME	Approximately 20 minutes
MATERIALS	Handout 55-1: Motivation
MINILECTURE	*An anonymous wit once remarked that statistics is a group of numbers looking for an argument. Whether we are looking for an argument or looking to avoid an argument, we need validation for the points we are making and the proposals we are offering. Today you will have an opportunity to gather statistics and to transfer them to a bar chart. Ideally, the numbers will be used to prove or disprove an assumption and thus win an argument.*

STEPS TO FOLLOW

1. Distribute Handout 55-1. Allow about 10 minutes for participants to complete it.

2. Appoint a leader who begins to tally the number of 1, 2, or 3 votes received for each item in Part B of the handout.

3. The leader then draws a bar chart to represent the tallies. The categories appear on the horizontal line, the *x*-axis, and the tallies appear as bars whose height corresponds to the numbers from 1 to 30 (or higher, depending on class size and votes) that appear on the vertical line (the *y*-axis).

DISCUSSION QUESTIONS

✓ Did the answers to questions 1 and 2 reveal any assumptions?

✓ What is a process in your organization that needs improving?

✓ What assumptions do you have about that process or what it needs to be improved?

✓ What data should be gathered around what critical aspects of the process?

✓ Discuss the impact on the Quality Council (or any audience) of having visual depictions instead of merely verbal.

✓ Discuss the charts we see daily—such as those in *USA Today*.

MOTIVATION

Directions: Begin by answering the first two questions in Part A. Then prioritize the remaining items in Part B, in terms of which motivate you the most. Do not change your answers to the first two questions as a result of working on the prioritization task.

Part A:

1. What one thing would make you like your job more? _____

2. What answer do you think most of the people in this room will give to question 1? _____

Part B:

Rank the following items, using 1 to indicate the thing that most motivates you to do your best work. Number 2 represents the second most important item, etc.

_____ Challenging tasks
_____ Having a good boss
_____ Pay raise
_____ Longer vacations
_____ Chance to participate in decisions
_____ Promotional opportunity
_____ Pay increase
_____ Socializing with co-workers
_____ Lack of pressure
_____ Proficiency in a small number of tasks

Put a star beside the items that received your 1, your 2, and your 3 vote. These are the items the leader uses in constructing a bar chart to reflect the most important motivators for class members.

OVERVIEW: PRESENTING TO THE QUALITY COUNCIL

As a general rule, teams make three presentations to the Quality Council:

1. In the very beginning as they lay out their intentions.

2. Again after they have gathered data and have decided how to proceed.

3. Finally, to report the results of their plan's implementation.

The team needs to make their presentation as persuasive as possible. So they must be prepared to show relevant data displayed on professional-looking graphs to support their request to change a process and to undertake a project and/or to solve a problem. The presentations generally run about a half-hour and almost never exceed an hour. They can be made by the team leader or by any other member(s) of the team. On occasion, the team's coach or mentor may briefly address the Council on behalf of the team.

Prior to the initial presentation to the Council, the team's coach plays an instrumental role in ensuring that the project the team wishes to pursue can be successful, given the limitations of their circumstances. The coach also helps them decide what resources are needed and what resources can be obtained. He/she guides the team past the project stage to the implementation stage: Assuming they have been successful with a pilot project, how extensively/effectively can the project be implemented throughout the organization?

In the initial presentation, the team is outlining their intended plan of action, justifying the need for resources to be allocated to this project, and demonstrating their belief that the project warrants the team's (and the Council's) attention. The Council needs assurance that the time required, usually three to six months, will be time well spent. They need evidence that the proposal being put forth truly supports the mission. Further, they need to see how the project supports the mission.

In each of the subsequent presentations to the Council, the team offers proof that they are thinking big and executing small. That is, they are aware of the organization's strategic plans, mission, vision, and value statements. The project they hope to undertake should have a direct link to the big picture, but should be small enough in scope that it is achievable within the time and money restraints teams inevitably face.

56

STATEMENTS OF INTENT

OBJECTIVE
To encourage development of a strong statement of intent for team **presentations to the Quality Council**

TIME
Approximately 15 minutes

MATERIALS
Handout 56-1: Repeated Themes

MINILECTURE
"Be accurate. Be brief. Be seated." These three guidelines serve you well in any type of presentation you are required to make.

STEPS TO FOLLOW
1. Allow teams of five or six participants about 10 minutes to complete the worksheet, the answers for which are:

1. Martin Luther King
2. Walter Cronkite
3. Arsenio Hall
4. Archie Bunker
5. Dan Quayle
6. Samuel Goldwyn
7. Woody Allen
8. Simone Signoret
9. Malcolm Forbes
10. Nikita Khrushchev

2. Call on each team to share their statements of intent.

DISCUSSION QUESTIONS
✓ Have you yet participated in team presentations to senior management? If so, what do you remember about them? If not, what factors do you think are the most important in determining your success?

✓ "Tell 'em what you're gonna tell 'em. Then, tell 'em. Then, tell 'em what you told 'em." This is standard advice for presenters. What other advice would you give to those selected to make presentations to senior management?

✓ Discuss the advantages and disadvantages of having a single person make the presentation, as opposed to several members of the team.

GAME STRETCHER

(10-20 minutes) Bring in a videotaped or written speech to see what themes or statements of intent are repeated. A classic is former Governor Mario Cuomo's address to the 1988 Democratic National Convention. In that speech he repeated the theme of family.

REPEATED THEMES

Directions: Can you identify the speaker of each of these famous signature lines?

1. _____ "I have a dream."
2. _____ "And that's the way it is."
3. _____ "Let's get busy."
4. _____ "It's a proven fact that capital punishment is a known deterrent against crime."
5. _____ "I stand by my misstatements."
6. _____ "A verbal agreement isn't worth the paper it's written on."
7. _____ "My one regret in life is that I am not someone else."
8. _____ "Nostalgia isn't what it used to be."
9. _____ "If you have a job without aggravation, you don't have a job."
10. _____ "Life is short; live it up."

The second half of the assignment asks you to think of a line that states a team's intent, a line that could be repeated at the beginning, middle, and end of the presentation. These statements of intent will probably not be clever or funny like most of those above. They will, however, state the team's focus or encapsulate the driving forces behind the team's work. An example might be, "We are primarily interested in reducing the number of errors." Or, "our primary goal is to increase customer satisfaction." If possible, use actual team projects to stimulate your thinking about the kind of statement that a Quality Council would be likely to remember.

_____

_____

_____

_____

_____

57

BREAKING SPEECH HABITS

OBJECTIVE

To help participants break the habit of saying "uh" when **making presentations**

TIME

Approximately 5 minutes

MATERIALS

Large sheets of paper (at least 8½ ∞ 11 inches)—one for each participant—on which you have printed in magic marker the word *Uh*

MINILECTURE

A habit has been described by Franklin Clark as "something you can do without thinking. Which is why, most of us have so many of them." We don't think much about our negative speech habits unless we have someone else assisting us to break them. We'll hear from at least one volunteer today as he/she talks about bosses. The speaker will receive feedback from us about any habits that should be broken. Is there someone who would like to share a few thoughts about bosses—the best or the worst you have ever had?

STEPS TO FOLLOW

1. Have the person leave the room for about 3 minutes to write down five words to describe the boss. [*Note:* If no one volunteers, make the subject even easier: "Talk to us a few minutes about how you got started in this field, about your family, about your favorite sports team."]

2. While the volunteer speaker is out of the room, distribute an "Uh" sheet to each person. Instruct them to wave it in the air each time they hear the speaker say the word *Uh*.

3. We can break old habits in about three weeks. Ask the speaker if such "shock therapy" could be continued for the next 20 days following this class. Who will shock him/her into breaking the "uh" habit?

DISCUSSION QUESTIONS

✓ What other annoying mannerisms should speakers try to eliminate?

✓ What factors increase the likelihood that a Quality Council will be persuaded to approve a team's plans?

58

THE PICK TECHNIQUE

OBJECTIVE

To provide participants an opportunity to have their ideas evaluated by a **Quality Council**

TIME

Approximately 35 minutes

MATERIALS

Transparency 58-1; optional: two prizes for volunteers

MINILECTURE

Ralph Waldo Emerson defined speech as power. Indeed, if your spoken ideas are accepted by influential others, you have exhibited the power to create a new reality. Today, you will have an opportunity to present your idea to others and to receive their feedback. The criteria they will use are these [show transparency].

STEPS TO FOLLOW

1. Allow participants about 5 minutes to outline an idea they feel would improve the organization in some way.

2. Select two volunteers and give them a moment or two to review their notes. As they do so, divide the rest of the class into teams of seven or eight and distribute nine assessment forms to each team. Have one person make a 5-minute presentation of an idea he or she thinks would benefit the organization. Then, as the class is working on their PICK assessments (individual assessments become a single group assessment), meet privately with the presenter to share feedback on his/her delivery.

3. Collect the PICK assessments (one from each group), hand them to the first presenter, and ask the second idea presenter to begin, while the groups undertake the same assessment.

DISCUSSION QUESTIONS

✓ We all have had good ideas for improving the organization in some way. What do you do with your good ideas?

✓ How can management ensure proper credit is given for those good ideas?

GAME STRETCHER

(10-60 minutes) Have each person present his/her idea and receive feedback from the PICK assessors.

P   What is the "*Project*"?

I   What "*Impact*" will it have?

C   What will the "*Costs*" be?

K   Should we "*Kick it*" off or out?

OVERVIEW:
CELEBRATING SUCCESS

Dr. Deming spoke often of the need for "joy in the workplace." He was not alone in advocating that the workplace should be a pleasant place to come to each day. This should be a place where important work is done, but done in an atmosphere of harmony, challenge, and interest. One way to create such a workplace is to celebrate the successes teams are bound to have. Such celebrations need not be expensive or complicated, but they should be *occurring*. Even if teams do not achieve their ultimate goal, they will have learned a great deal along the way, and such learning is in itself a cause for celebration.

Teams initially come together with individual members asking the "WIFM" question: "What's in it for me?" If they are successful, the teams then progress to the WIFTO question: "What's in it for the organization?" Their personal concerns recede as the larger, organizational concerns come to dominate the team's work. As this happens, of course, a collective mindset, dominated by a singular purpose, dominates the team's thinking and acting. They come to regard one another as members of a special unit, often demonstrating the concern and conviviality that family members show to one another.

In this spirit of cooperation it is not hard to find reasons to celebrate. The team leader ensures that the celebratory occasions are appropriate in number (neither excessive nor overly limited). The celebrations need not be costly or lengthy, but they should be deliberate and well timed. Whenever the team meets a milestone or has a successful presentation to the Council or whenever they complete an especially arduous task, the leader should arrange for some sort of recognition.

Internal celebrations are critical for sustaining the team's momentum, but there should also be external celebrations from time to time. The external celebration should be prompted by those outside the team. The coach or mentor, the manager, or even the members of the Council, as the circumstances warrant, should recognize the members of the team and give them deserved attention.

59

EPONYMS FOR EXCELLENCE

OBJECTIVE   To promote **celebration of team success** via eponyms for individual excellence

TIME   Approximately 10 minutes

MATERIALS   None

MINILECTURE   *Don Petersen, former CEO of Ford, maintains that "results depend on relationships." His words have special significance for teams, whose members depend on each other for collective success. Once the successes have been realized—at any stage of the team's journey—they should be celebrated.*

Eponyms are one way to celebrate the individual excellence on which team success depends. An eponym is a person's name that stands for the accomplishment or act the person is known for. As an example, Dr. F. A. Mesmer had a hypnotic stare; hence "to mesmerize." The Earl of Sandwich, of course, created a food item in the late 1700s that we still enjoy today. Occasionally, you will hear someone in a Quality environment use Vilfredo Pareto's name—not for the Pareto Chart but as a verb: "Let's Pareto it."

STEPS TO FOLLOW   **1.** Divide the class into groups of four or five. They may opt to use their own names or the names of people on their regular process improvement teams.

2. Based on what they know of one another (or of the people in their regular work teams), they create eponyms—words that have a particular meaning based on the personality or characteristics of the individual. What would it mean if they, for example, "pulled a Kristi" or if they decide to "Sam this."

DISCUSSION QUESTIONS   ✓ In what other ways can individuals be recognized for both their singular and their collective contributions?

✓ What would you like to be remembered for?

60

SHOW AND SWELL

OBJECTIVE To provide a vehicle by which team members can self-recognize their **contributions to the team**

TIME Approximately 20 minutes (longer for a larger class)

MATERIALS None

MINILECTURE *Quality guru Philip Crosby advocates having "show and tell" days so teams can celebrate their successes. Assume that your team has been invited to participate in such a day. The letter of invitation has asked that each person spend one minute telling others about his or her special talents, skills, knowledge, or abilities. What would each of you have to say? What is so unique about you that you swell with pride when you think about what you can accomplish or have accomplished? We each have special gifts but we do not usually declare them publicly. Today, I hope, you will. As you do so, remind yourselves you are the quality grains and the quality stones of which George Bernard Shaw speaks: "Grain by grain—a loaf; stone upon stone—a palace."*

STEPS TO FOLLOW

1. Permit participants about 5 minutes to prepare a one minute show and tell talk extolling their own virtues.

2. Allow time for each person who wishes to make the presentation. Encourage brief applause following each presentation.

DISCUSSION QUESTIONS

✓ If you were to plan an actual show and tell day for your organization, what would the plans include?

✓ In what ways other than monetary can the organization recognize the work of teams?

✓ How meaningful are Employee of the Month programs?

✓ Some organizations are beginning to include families of honorees in success celebrations. How do you feel about this?

✓ Team leaders can arrange unofficial minicelebrations at most team meetings. These minicelebrations are small gestures that celebrate (team) life itself. What might some of these be?

TEAM MEETINGS

The team meeting is the heart and soul of the Quality world. You can have an enlightened CEO, empowering managers, receptive employees, a conscientious Quality Council and all the resources in the world. But if the team is not meeting on a regular basis, the important work of improving processes is not being done.

All too often, employees feel that because they have attended so many meetings in their lifetime, they know what constitutes meeting excellence. Nothing could be further from the truth. Until you have read every book and magazine article that tells how to make your meetings better, then you still have something to learn.

This section provides practice in using the tools and techniques employed by those who have achieved mastery in running team meetings.

OVERVIEW: TASK FUNCTIONS

At any given moment, while members sit in attendance at a team meeting, they are engaged in one of two types of behavior:

✓ Either a behavior that advances or retards the movement toward task accomplishment.

✓ Or a behavior that advances or retards the group's harmony.

Task behaviors focus on progressing toward the ultimate outcome. They include such things as sticking to the agenda, asking for clarification, assigning tasks, conducting brainstorming, etc. If members do not contribute or if they contribute in a negative way (such as when they use sarcasm instead of constructive feedback), they are displaying negative task behaviors. When they summarize or point out an oversight or lead the team to consensus, they are engaging in positive task behaviors.

By virtue of their presence on the team, members have implicitly pledged their desire to have the team succeed. This success depends on the synergy created by the individual releases of positive energy. That energy derives from their attention to the task.

Employees in Quality conscious organizations—unlike employees of the past—really have two jobs. They have to do the job they were hired to do. They also have the job of improving the quality of their work processes and their work outputs. To that end, teams are formed. Employees are expected to give themselves as fully to that job as to the job specified in their position descriptions. To those who ask, "How will I find time to attend meetings concerned with improving quality?" the answer usually given is, "Quality *is* your job."

While it is admittedly difficult to find time in the beginning, the time and money that teams save by the end of their projects almost always provides a worthwhile return on the initial investment.

It is important for the team leader to remind the team occasionally of the payoff their work has for the organization. Task accomplishment is often tedious work, but without it there is no success. As members behave in a task-conscious fashion, the leader or facilitator should note their contributions periodically.

61

TASKED BEHAVIORS

OBJECTIVE

To provide an opportunity to practice a **task behavior** at a **team meeting**

TIME

Approximately 40 minutes

MATERIALS

Transparency 61-1: Task Behaviors; Handout 61-1: Observer's Form—one for each person

MINILECTURE

Leadership of a team typically resides in one person. At any given moment, however, that leadership may be briefly shared with a motivated team member or with the facilitator. Be reminded of Steve Miller's comment, "Great leaders get extraordinary things done in organizations by inspiring and motivating others toward a common purpose." Here are some of the task behaviors team leaders/members engage in. [Show transparency.]

STEPS TO FOLLOW

1. Ask participants to select one of the task behaviors—one that they typically do not do in meetings. Ask half of them to tell one other person (their partner) what that behavior is. [Advise the half doing the telling that they are expected to gain some practice with that behavior in an upcoming meeting.]

2. Distribute Handout 61-1 to the partners. [*Note:* If one person is left over, he/she should join you in observing the group process as a whole.] The partners watch their individual team members in a meeting; they look to see if the member is trying to do the thing he/she does not usually do in meetings.

3. Ask each person who selected a behavior to sit in a circle near the front of the room. Their partners sit or stand outside the circle, located so that they can watch their task behavior role playing partner who is inside the circle. Essentially, those on the outside watch their partners carefully to note the extent to which they are trying to engage in the role behavior that they do not typically engage in. Those on the inside, of course, participate in a meeting (and try to improve a behavior).

4. Ask the inner group to appoint a leader and to discuss this question:

   The City Council has asked you, as a representative group of businesspeople, to advise them on the issue of panhandling. In short, they want your advice: Should beggars or homeless people be allowed to solicit money from passersby on the street?

   You will have 15 minutes to reach consensus.

5. After 15 minutes, say, "Time's up." Ask for their recommendation, and then ask that they return to their seats with their partners, who give them feedback on whether they practiced the behavior they said they needed to practice. Then give your observations about the meeting in general.

6. The process is repeated. Ask the outside observing partners to select one behavior from the transparency [show it now]. The original members now act as the partners to observe whether team members are gaining practice with the task behavior they would like to become more skilled with. [Give each outsider partner an Observer's Form now.]

7. Once the group is assembled, give them this topic and allow time afterwards for observations to be shared. [They will appoint a leader.]

> The President has asked for your advice as a representative group of taxpaying citizens. You and the members of your focus group have 15 minutes to decide this issue:

> Should we continue with our foreign aid policy as it now exists or should we allocate more or less than we do? Also, should we continue giving aid to countries who are long standing recipients? (Israel, for example, receives nearly a third of the $14.5 billion we expend each year and Egypt receives $2.5 billion.)

8. As before, they receive feedback from their partners and then the whole team receives general feedback from you as the observer.

DISCUSSION QUESTIONS

✓ In what ways do teams waste time at meetings?

✓ Discuss this saying in relation to expanding your repertoire of team meeting skills: "If you always do what you've always done, you'll always be what you've always been."

✓ What new behaviors have you adopted in relation to work or team meetings?

✓ What new behaviors do you think you should adopt as a result of this exercise?

TASK BEHAVIORS

Offer suggestions.

Help team stick to the agenda.

Ask for clarification.

Assign tasks.

Conduct brainstorming.

Synthesize.

Make note of time.

Help members reach consensus.

Review progress.

Volunteer for assignments.

Ask questions.

Serve as recorder.

Summarize.

Offer feedback.

Keep team focused on topic.

Bring up new business.

Come to meetings prepared.

OBSERVER'S FORM

As you watch your partner engage in a short meeting, note whether he/she is practicing the behavior he/she told you would be developed. Make your notes here and then share them privately with your partner when the meeting has been concluded.

1. Was time being wasted in the selection of a leader? Explain. If so, did your partner do anything to move the meeting along?

_____

_____

_____

_____

_____

2. What did your partner actually *do* in this meeting?

_____

_____

_____

_____

_____

3. What was his or her greatest contribution?

_____

_____

_____

_____

_____

4. What advice would you give your partner to develop his/her potential as far as future team meetings are concerned?

_____

_____

_____

_____

_____

62

SYNTHESIS

OBJECTIVE

To give participants the opportunity to develop their **synthesizing skill for use in team meetings**

TIME

Approximately 10 minutes

MATERIALS

Handout 62-1: Synchronous Synthesis; optional prize

MINILECTURE

The ability to synthesize information is a high-level thinking skill. It requires taking ideas that appear to be unrelated and finding a relationship or connecting purpose among them. It requires fast thinking and allows you to respond with poise to unexpected utterances at meetings. Think of it this way: "To be open-minded, active-memoried, and persistently experimental." (That is how Leon Stein describes an intelligent person, and the ability to synthesis is surely an intellectual skill.)

STEPS TO FOLLOW

1. Distribute handouts and allow 5 minutes for participants to synthesize at least three disparate combinations. [*Optional:* Award a prize to the first person who is able to do so.]

2. Call on several participants to share their answers.

DISCUSSION QUESTIONS

✓ Many people have difficulty assimilating information and then drawing logical conclusions or spotting possible trends in relation to that information. The information remains isolated rather than synthesized. Apart from the fact that we may not have received cognitive skills training, why do you think the skill of synthesizing is a skill many people lack?

✓ How can organizations encourage employees to think of the big picture?

GAME STRETCHER

(5 minutes) Have participants write down three words (one on each of three notecards). Collect the cards, mix them up, and walk around the room, distributing two to each participant. Ask them to use both words they received to create a statement related to Total Quality.

SYNCHRONOUS SYNTHESIS

Directions: We call this exercise "synchronous" because you all do it at the same time. The task involves synthesis—the ability to see a connection in seemingly unrelated material. As a team member, you can make a valuable contribution if you possess this skill. Not everyone is able to step back, consider what has been done or is being done, and then make a relevant observation concerning it.

You will work individually to take a pair of words and relate them to team meetings or team assignments. For example, if the two words were *ostrich* and *umbrella*, your synthesizing statement might be this:

> We have a challenging task before us. I know there is a temptation among some of us to hide our head in the sand, like an *ostrich,* and hope this problem will go away. But it won't. We've been charged with finding a solution. We've been asked to develop a mission statement. This should be broad enough to serve as an *umbrella,* covering every employee in every department.

As soon as you have developed synthesizing statements for three pairs of words, raise your hand.

1. question — dates
2. coffee — minister
3. tape — heart
4. printer — brick
5. label — postage
6. home — gazelle
7. cord — Cadillac
8. Deming — travel
9. mosque — priority
10. holiday — rubber band

63

VOLUNTEERING

OBJECTIVE   To encourage **participation by team members**

TIME   Approximately 10 minutes

MATERIALS   Two token prizes, nicely wrapped (kept out of sight)

MINILECTURE   *I need a volunteer.* [Go to steps one and two now.]

[Continued] *Where would America be without our volunteers? We see them everywhere—in hospitals, in schools, in libraries, in youth centers—sacrificing their time to make their corner of the world a better place. We need volunteers on teams as well, people who take on tasks that need to be done. Such individuals reflect John Wise's definition of altruism: "Making the common good the mark of one's aim." So-and-so here* [give name of person who volunteered] *was willing to help me out, even though he didn't know what he was getting into. For that, I think he deserves a round of applause.* [Initiate clapping.] *He did not know there was any prize involved and yet he was willing to take action for the common good. Does anyone here do any volunteer work in his or her community?* [Allow a few moments for members to discuss their volunteering experiences.]

We are going to engage in a team-related activity now. Before we begin, though, I need a volunteer. [Reach for the second prize as you say this. Then continue with step 3.]

STEPS TO FOLLOW

1. Wait until a volunteer raises his/her hand. (If someone asks what for, say that the job is an easy one.)

2. As soon as someone has volunteered, thank him or her and make a big show of going over to hand the person a prize. As you do so, say, "To thank you for volunteering, I have a prize here. You are free to give it to anyone within four feet of your chair." [Allow a few moments for laughter and the actual giving away of the prize. Say something like, "John knows it is better to give than receive, don't you, John?" Then continue with the minilecture.]

3. It will be interesting to see who, if anyone volunteers now—as the class probably thinks they will have to give their prize away. This time, however, you allow the volunteer to keep the prize. Then advise him/her that you really do not need a volunteer: The whole point of this exercise was to see if anyone *would* volunteer, thinking they would probably have to give the prize away. The person who does truly has concern for the common good.

✓ For what kinds of tasks are volunteers typically needed on teams?

✓ What can a leader do if no one is volunteering?

✓ What might the lack of volunteers be telling the leader?

✓ Should the leader or facilitator reward the volunteer in any way other than verbally?

OVERVIEW: MAINTENANCE FUNCTIONS

Maintenance functions are related to the people performing the task, as opposed to the task itself. Although the facilitator and team leader share the primary responsibility for ensuring smooth relations, any team member may exhibit at any time a behavior that promotes harmony and a cordial working relationship.

Any team that is too task-oriented finds friction erupting from time to time. Admirable though it is to focus exclusively on the work to be done, team members lose interest in the team's operation over time if there is not enough human interest to make the team's work markedly different from their regular work. Creating that interest is the responsibility of both the team leader and the facilitator—and even, as called for, individual team members.

Team work is distinguished from individual work in that it is a collective effort to solve a particular problem. The work is neither repetitive nor prescribed. In fact, the team often becomes the prescribing force for the changes to be enacted in future work processes. The team has a finite life. Once their work is completed, they return to their regular jobs. But for the duration of their time together, they should be able to look forward to pleasant relationships, challenging assignments, and hard but rewarding work.

Maintenance behaviors for a team are like maintenance behaviors for mechanical equipment. They keep the team's operation running smoothly. They prevent breakdowns in the team's communication and cooperative processes—just as maintenance procedures help equipment to run smoothly.

Maintenance behaviors include such actions as ensuring that all opinions are heard, providing feedback, smoothing ruffled feathers, complimenting or showing appreciation of individual and team efforts, allowing time for humor or socializing, demonstrating respect, etc.

All work and no play may make Jack a dull boy, but all work and no harmony make teams nonfunctional.

64

MAINTAINING BEHAVIORS

OBJECTIVE   To provide an opportunity to practice a **maintenance behavior** at a **team meeting**

TIME   Approximately 40 minutes

MATERIALS   Transparency 64-1: Maintenance Behaviors; Handout 64-1: Observer's Form—one for each person

MINILECTURE   *Oscar Blumenthal defines sociability is "the art of unlearning to be preoccupied with yourself." When you engage in maintenance behaviors, you are preoccupying yourself with others. You exhibit concern for their well-being, knowing full well that team meetings cannot be fully successful if teams concentrate only on the task. Here are some of the maintenance behaviors team leaders/members engage in.* [Show transparency.]

STEPS TO FOLLOW
1. Ask participants to select a maintenance behavior that they typically do *not* do in meetings. Ask half of them each to tell *one other person* (their partner) what that behavior is. [Advise the half doing the telling that they will be expected to practice that behavior in an upcoming meeting.]

2. Distribute Handout 64-1 to the partners now. [*Note:* If one person is left over, he/she should join you as an observer of the group process as a whole.] The partners watch their individual team members in a meeting; they see whether the members are trying to do the thing they do *not* usually do in meetings.

3. Ask each person who selected a behavior to sit in a circle near the front of the room. Their partners sit or stand outside the circle, located so that they can watch their maintenance behavior role playing partner who is inside the circle. Essentially, those on the outside watch their partners carefully to note the extent to which they are trying to engage in their selected role behaviors. Those on the inside, of course, participate in a meeting.

4. Ask them to appoint their own leader and to discuss this question:

    The secretaries in your organization have asked that something special be done to honor them in April, National Secretaries Month. Management has turned the request over to your ad hoc team and has allowed a budget of $500. You have 15 minutes to reach consensus regarding how that money should be spent.

5. After 15 minutes, say, "Time's up." Ask for their recommendation, and then ask that they return to their seats with their partners, who give them feedback on whether they practiced the behaviors they said they needed to practice. Then give your observations about the meeting in general.

6. The process is repeated. Ask the outside observing partners to select one behavior each from the transparency [show it now]. The original members now act as the partner to observe whether the team members are practicing the selected maintenance behaviors. [Give each an Observer's Form now.]

7. Once the group is assembled, give them this topic and allow time for observations to be shared. [They appoint their own leader.]

Senior management wants everyone to have training in "effective team meetings." The problem is that the training budget has already been committed, most of it going to classes for the new computer system being installed. Your team has been asked to come up with five viable ways to ensure that training on effective meetings can be given to every employee. Your budget is limited to $1000. You have 15 minutes to accomplish your task.

DISCUSSION QUESTIONS

✓ Are you a task-oriented or people-oriented worker? What are the pros and cons of each orientation?

✓ Think about less than successful meetings you have attended in the last three months. What caused the team to be less effective than they might have been?

✓ What is one thing every meeting should have?

MAINTENANCE BEHAVIORS

Compliment the team & individual members.

Encourage each person to speak.

Ensure members treat one another respectfully.

Use humor.

Take a personal interest in the lives of others.

Suggest a break if necessary.

Ask if everyone agrees.

Use an icebreaker.

Ensure there is common understanding before moving along.

Reduce defensive behavior.

Watch body language to spot possible problems.

Attend to physical comfort.

Develop pride in team success.

Encourage the team.

OBSERVER'S FORM

As you watch your partner engage in a short meeting, note whether he/she is practicing the behavior he/she told you would be developed. Make your notes here and then share them privately with your partner when the meeting has concluded.

1. Did the leader or your observee do anything to warm up the group before beginning the task?

_____

_____

_____

_____

_____

2. What did your partner actually *do* in this meeting?

_____

_____

_____

_____

_____

3. What was his/her greatest contribution?

_____

_____

_____

_____

_____

4. What advice would you give your partner to develop his/her potential in future team meetings?

_____

_____

_____

_____

_____

65

INDIVIDUAL TALENTS

OBJECTIVE

To demonstrate the positive feelings associated with knowing one's **individual talents are integral to the team success**

TIME

Approximately 20 minutes

MATERIALS

Flip chart and marking pen; 30 to 40 small sheets of paper (3 ∞ 2), for each table group

MINILECTURE

We all need to feel that our skills have value to the organization. In a general sense, our value is reaffirmed each time we receive a paycheck, for if we were not able to do the job we probably would not have the job. More specifically, we appreciate hearing from time to time that our talents are appreciated. I, for example, am awfully good with math. I believe, as does James Sylvester, that mathematics is "the music of reason." I listen to that music and if I were on your team, I would be the person you would call on if data needed to be analyzed. Let me show you just how good I am with numbers.

Would one of you mind working with me? [Wait for volunteer and station him/her at the flip chart at a location that allows the class to see what is being written but prevents you from seeing anything.] *Could you write a number with three different digits, but don't let me see it. Now go ahead and reverse those numbers. Subtract the smaller one from the larger one. Do you have a three-digit difference?* [If yes, then continue.] *If you give me either the first or the last number in the difference, I will be able to give you the whole remainder. All I need is one number—the first or the last digit—to get me started.* [After getting the number, ask if it is the first or the last digit.]

[Note: Naturally, there is a gimmick. The three-digit difference always has 9 as the middle number, and the other two numbers always add up to 9. So, no matter what number they give you, all you have to do is subtract that number from 9. If they give you 3 as the first digit, the answer is 396. Again, 9 is always in the middle and the other two numbers add up to 9.

Now if they told you the difference had only *two* digits, the answer is always 99. The person who has a two-digit answer does not have to give you one part of it.

Of course, you should make a show of figuring out the number. Furrow your brow, count on your fingers, then snap your fingers, and smile broadly once you have "figured out" the answer.]

1. After your demonstration, ask participants to write down what the[y] is their most outstanding talent or trait.

2. Have each person join five or six others, and distribute five or [six] sheets of paper to *each* person. [*Note:* If participants are seated it is easier simply to place a pile of paper in the center of the table and let each person reach for his/her own as needed. Each person needs the same number of sheets as there are people at the table.]

3. Say, "Let's start with _____ at this table. [Choose one person at each table as a starting point.] As you look at him/her and as you consider what you have learned about this person since the class started, write down on the small sheet of paper what you feel the person's most outstanding talent is. If you have the advantage of knowing the person before the class began, you of course will be even closer in your estimate of his or her abilities. Fold the paper up and give it to _____ [an appointed collector]."

4. Have the individuals who were the first objects of the talent guessing process, unfold the five or six sheets of paper they received and briefly report to the class how they feel about the talents *others* believe they possess.

5. Continue until every person in each group has had the same opportunity to receive feedback and report on the accuracy of that feedback to the members of their group.

DISCUSSION QUESTIONS

✓ Why is what people perceive about our skills so often at odds with what we know or believe?

✓ Given the fact that there is probably little congruency, how can we learn more about, and tap into, the tremendous potential to be found in the workplace?

66

'TWAS THE FRIGHT BEFORE CHRISTMAS

OBJECTIVE
To encourage **maintenance behaviors** that reflect understanding of the fact that team members' psychological and physical comfort impacts team effort

TIME
Approximately 10 minutes

MATERIALS
Handout 66-1

MINILECTURE
When team members feel excluded, they are not likely to participate as willingly in the team's work. One factor that leads to such feelings is language. If members feel overwhelmed by unfamiliar language, they may think they should not be part of the team. It is important for those concerned with maintenance behaviors to ensure a common understanding of the terms used.

Mark Hopkins asserts that "language is the picture and counterpart of thought." As an effective team member or team leader, you must use language in such a way that others can see the same picture you have in your head—use it in such a way that your thoughts become clear to others. Let me show you how difficult or inappropriate vocabulary can prevent the message from getting through and leave participants feeling confused and perhaps isolated.

METHOD
Divide the class into teams of two or three and distribute the handout. Once they figure out what is being said [the familiar passage, "'Twas the night before Christmas and all through the house"], segue into the discussion questions.

DISCUSSION QUESTIONS
✓ Are people in your organization speaking the "common language of quality"? If so, what steps were taken to make this happen? If not, what could be done to develop this understanding?

✓ How could those interested in improving their vocabulary work within the organization to make that improvement?

✓ Describe the communications emanating from upper management.

HANDOUT

Directions: As you read the following admittedly difficult passage, try to understand the point b
Once you have figured out the message, write it in the space beneath the passage. Do *not* share your answer.

It was the nocturnal segment of the diurnal period preceding the annual celebratory observance of the emergence of a deified persona gratis into the mundane entity, and throughout the domicile that is shared by individuals bearing verisimilitude in the appellations that make them cohesive, kinetic perambulations were not in evidence among the possessors of this potential, nor were they evident in that species of domestic carnivores bearing the cognomen of *mus musculus*. Synthetic appurtenances for extreme appendages were meticulously suspended from the forward edge of a carbonaceous-related caloric apparatus, pursuant to our anticipatory hedonism regarding the imminent advent of an eccentric, canonized philanthropist among whose folkloric appellations is the allusion to a "caged" male individual who starred in a cinematic production, the title of which refers to being assaulted by a lunar body, and the female star of which is known by a monosyllabic name.

Translation: _____

_____

_____

_____

_____

_____

_____

_____

_____

_____

_____

_____

_____

_____

_____

_____

_____

_____

_____

_____

OVERVIEW: IMPROVING THE MEETING PROCESS

Like all other work processes, the meeting process can be improved. No matter how efficiently a team's meetings are being run, they can be run even more efficiently. Whenever a team acquires a new tool, discovers a new means of building consensus, or benchmarks to find new meeting methods, it is improving the process. Not every tool, means, or method works for every team but surely some of them do.

Here are a few suggestions for meeting improvement. As you review them, think about the last team meeting you attended. Which of these were used at that meeting? (Check them off.)

- [ ] Listing beside the agenda items the amount of time to be spent on each topic.
- [ ] Charging money by the minute for latecomers.
- [ ] Holding meetings at the end of the day so that team members—eager to leave—do not waste time.
- [ ] Inviting experts in as needed to address the team.
- [ ] Celebrating periodically.
- [ ] Having the ground rules printed, laminated, and posted in the meeting room.
- [ ] Starting at an unusual time—8:10 instead of 8:00—which tends to promote promptness.
- [ ] Keeping a notebook of lessons learned to help the next team.

The meeting process should be evaluated periodically. In addition to an evaluation form, the team can assess the cost of a one- or two-hour meeting in terms of the hourly cost of having eight or ten people in a room. (Don't forget the related cost of fringe benefits for the team members.) Once that figure is obtained, the members should ask themselves if their accomplishments during that meeting matched the cost of the meeting. Would their customers agree that the money was well spent?

Here's a general rule for operating efficient meetings:

	focus	attention		goal		effort.
Do	direct	time	**re:**	purpose	**of collective team**	capability.
	insist on	interest		mission		value.
				benefits		output.

67

(UNDER) GROUND RULES

OBJECTIVE	To provide participants with an introductory exercise for the **first team meeting**
TIME	Approximately 10 minutes
MATERIALS	Flip chart and marking pen
MINILECTURE	*Arnold Toynbee has labeled familiarity as "the opiate of the imagination." Within the workplace, those processes, practices, and procedures that we know well sometimes "drug" us and prevent us from looking at the process in a new way. Each of you will be a team member or team leader before you retire. It will be important—especially at the first meeting of a new team—to encourage original thought.*
	I'm going to share with you an example of how a familiar form can look unfamiliar if parts of it are taken away. This new form may create new thoughts. The same is true in the workplace. Reengineers often ask a question such as, "If we had to remove 66 percent of the steps in this process, what would the new process look like?"
	I'm going to show you part of a word with 55 percent of the original removed. Your task is to figure out the word. I'll even make it a little easier for you: The letters missing from the front of the word are the same letters missing from the end of the word. What is the word?
METHOD	Write these letters on the flip chart so that everyone can see them: *ergro*. Allow about 5 minutes for participants to figure out the word. (The answer is *underground*.)
DISCUSSION QUESTIONS	✓ What processes in your own organization do you wish you could start from scratch?
	✓ Have you removed any nonvalue-added steps from your own work?
GAME STRETCHER	(5 minutes) Undertake the same exercise with various other words.

68

FUNCTIONAL AND FRIVOLOUS

OBJECTIVE To encourage the development of **ground rules for team meetings**

TIME Approximately 20 minutes

MATERIALS Two flip charts (if possible); marking pens, including two red ones

MINILECTURE *Businesspeople are typically, and perhaps rightfully, cynical about meetings. In fact, there is a sign by an anonymous wit in the meeting room of one American firm: "Meetings are no substitute for progress." One thing that helps meetings to run smoothly and team members to accomplish a great deal is a set of groundrules.*

STEPS TO FOLLOW
1. Ask participants to divide a sheet of paper into two columns. In the left column, they should write one functional groundrule that will make meetings more efficient. In the right column, they should write one frivolous grounds rule, such as, "Only Ms. Fields' chocolate cookies can be served as a refreshment."

2. Collect their papers.

3. Divide the class in half and assemble each half around a flip chart. Give one group half the papers, and ask them to write down only the functional grounds rules, avoiding duplicates. Have the other group, given the other half of the papers, record only the frivolous grounds rules. When both groups have finished, have them exchange their sets of papers and continue with the listing, again eliminating duplicates.

4. When they are finished, switch the flip charts. The teams place red stars beside 10 usable ideas.

DISCUSSION QUESTIONS
✓ In what ways can the meeting leader use the posted grounds rules?
✓ What should the grounds rules say about voting?

174

69

MEETING ASSESSMENT

OBJECTIVE   To have participants develop a **meeting assessment** form

TIME   Approximately 15 minutes

MATERIALS   None

MINILECTURE   *The Quality movement advocates continuous improvement. In the spirit of continuous improvement, many team leaders seek feedback on how they can make future meetings better. Such leaders feel they have failed if they hear comments such as this by Herm Staudt: "I always come to meetings with a problem. I always leave with a briefing and a problem."*

One large company encourages managers to distribute evaluation forms to participants at the end of meetings. The managers are free to write any questions they wish on the form. One manager prefers just a single-question assessment. His evaluation form reads, "If you didn't have to come to this meeting, would you have?" The monosyllabic responses speak volumes. You will now work in small groups to prepare an evaluation form that you can use when you return to work.

STEPS TO FOLLOW
1. Divide the class into teams of six or seven.
2. Have them prepare an evaluation form that is both probing and user-friendly.
3. Ask whether any team would like to share what they have.

DISCUSSION QUESTIONS
✓ What can be done to improve the meetings in your department?
✓ What causes waste in the meetings you attend?
✓ What should a meeting agenda look like and when should attendees receive it? How closely should it be followed?

GAME STRETCHER   Ask for a volunteer to type the evaluation forms and submit copies to all attendees.

SECTION 9

PROBLEM-SOLVING TOOLS

Both individuals in a Quality environment and teams need to expand their repertoire of problem-solving skills. The tools that served us in the past may not be adequate for the present, and they may be totally inappropriate for the future. As Albert Einstein observed, "We live in a world of problems which can no longer be solved by the level of thinking which created them."

This section is designed to refine existing tools, as well as to develop the new tools that individuals and team members need as they continuously work to improve processes.

OVERVIEW: TOOLS OF THE SCIENTIFIC APPROACH

The Quality movement in America was started, many believe, by the statistician Dr. Walter Shewhart, a mentor of Dr. W. Edwards Deming. Consequently, a strong metrics thread is woven throughout the tapestry we know as Quality.

The push for data-driven decisions is an example of this dependence on the scientific approach. The specific tools used by quality improvement teams include the scatter diagram, the fishbone diagram, the histogram, the Pareto chart, and force-field analysis. These familiar tools are explored, but the control charts used to ascertain variation in manufacturing processes are not (these are beyond the scope and intent of this book).

Nonetheless, specificity is encouraged in the work of teams. For example, as quality advocates in a manufacturing environment consider the operating time of specific processes, they gather data about the six big losses:

1. Equipment failure.

2. Set-up and adjustment time.

3. Number of defective outputs.

4. Losses from yield.

5. Stops.

6. Reduced speed losses.

No matter what process—industrial or service—is being studied, the team should have a sense of what constitutes the big losses. The losses occur in every phase of the transformation from input to output. Each department—production, operations, sales, customer service—should be able to isolate work that is not optimized.

The general scientific approach applies to the general work of teams:

Identify the problem; generate solutions; select the most workable solution; apply it; assess the results; institutionalize the results if positive; select another solution (or adjust the original) if not. Within this general framework, specific approaches are applied to specific offshoots of the problem.

To illustrate, the second stage in general problem solving is the generation of possible solutions. Brainstorming can be used to obtain the list of ideas. So can stratification, "what-if" questions, or the "blue sky" scenario, which asks team members to imagine the best possible outcome for the existing problem. Similarly, each of the other stages involves a plethora of information gathering techniques. The more tools that leaders/facilitators possess, the richer the team's contribution can be.

70

THE SHEWHART CYCLE: PDCA

OBJECTIVE

To introduce participants to the full meaning of **PDCA**

TIME

Approximately 10 minutes

MATERIALS

Chart paper and marking pens

MINILECTURE

Dr. Walter Shewhart formulated the PDCA cycle, later modified by his student, Dr. W. Edwards Deming as the PDS [for "study"] A cycle. The letters, which stand for plan, do, check, act, are easy to remember. However, despite their simplicity, the letters represent substantial amounts of work by team members. Planning is the most critical for, as George Hewell wryly observes, "People who fail to plan, have planned to fail." Solid preparation in the first stage facilitates doing in the second.

STEPS TO FOLLOW

1. Divide the class into four groups, and distribute chart paper and marking pens to each.

2. Assign each a letter: P, D, C, or A. Ask them to define what is meant by planning, doing, checking, and acting.

Typical answers for planning include: Selecting the problem, defining the problem, analyzing the problem, generating possible solutions, gathering data related to the problem, selecting a solution to implement, planning how the selected solution will be implemented.

Typical answers for doing include: Seeking permission from the Quality Council to proceed, advising those who will be affected by the change, gathering baseline data, implementing the plan.

Typical answers for checking include: Talking to those affected by the change, gathering data on the effects of the change, analyzing the data, presenting the data to the Quality Council.

Typical answers for acting include: Making calibrations to the original plan, presenting the results to the Quality Council and seeking approval to take next steps, institutionalizing the plan.

3. Post the work and refer to it as later problems are solved.

DISCUSSION QUESTIONS

✓ Why do you think Dr. Deming preferred to call the third step study instead of check?

✓ How are possible solutions usually generated in your team meetings?

✓ Is your team overly dependent on brainstorming?

✓ What other idea-generation techniques do you use?

✓ While the planning stage is the most complex, the doing stage is usually the most difficult. What advice would you give to teams at that stage to facilitate the doing process?

✓ What resources exist in your organization to help you with the checking process?

✓ Whose help should you enlist when you are ready for the acting stage?

GAME STRETCHER   (5 minutes) Have participants create a four-letter term for the problem-solving approach that their organization uses.

71

EXPLOSION/IMPLOSION FOR PROBLEM SOLVING

OBJECTIVE

To help participants understand the fully scrutiny required by the **scientific approach to problem solving**

TIME

Approximately 15 minutes

MATERIALS

Handout 71-1: Explode/Implode Steps of the Scientific Approach

MINILECTURE

"A problem," according to Henry J. Kaiser, "is an opportunity in work clothes." Long and hard efforts—both mental and physical—precede solutions. Part of that work requires us to look at the steps in the scientific approach from two perspectives: the explosion of possibilities and the implosion of possibilities. Handout 71-1 tells more.

STEPS TO FOLLOW

1. Divide the class into pairs and distribute the handout. (A leftover person can be your partner or can work alone to create an mnemonic device for the six steps of the scientific approach.)

2. Call on a few pairs at random to share their ideas.

DISCUSSION QUESTIONS

✓ Think of a problem facing your department or your organization.

✓ Now think of the six steps to the scientific approach. Which step is the most difficult to implement as far as this problem is concerned?

✓ What problem solving skills have you acquired in high school and/or college?

✓ Are decisions/problems in your work unit typically made or solved by the scientific approach? Why or why not? If they are not, which approach *is* used?

GAME STRETCHER

(15–30 minutes) Have each pair join another pair to create a composite set of explosion/implosion guidelines. If time permits, have them share their composites with another four-person team to create a supercomposite. Depending on the size of the class, super-supercomposites could be created.

EXPLODE/IMPLODE STEPS OF THE SCIENTIFIC APPROACH

Directions: Listed below are the steps in the scientific approach to problem solving. There are two columns beside each step. For the first column, list questions or actions that *might* be asked/taken to *expand* the step. Your partner lists questions or actions that *might* be asked/taken to *narrow* the scope of the step.

This is actually a problem solving technique within a problem-solving technique. Explode with ideas and then refine that explosion. Pull the ideas back until you have isolated the best or most workable one. One idea has been provided in each column for each step to start you out. For each step, try to come up with two ideas in each column. (Use additional paper.)

Step	Explosion	Implosion
1. Define problem.	Check with senior management.	Run the final selection by the team's coach.
2. Analyze the problem.	Get input from customers.	Select the primary cause.
3. Generate ideas.	Ask nonteam members for additional ideas.	Prioritize the most usable.
4. Plan.	What are the costs?	Establish criteria.
5. Implement the plan.	What data verify success or failure?	Decide on the next steps.
6. Assess the worth of the plan.	What could we have done differently?	Should we try again?

72

DEFINING THE PROBLEM: REALLY AND IDEALLY

OBJECTIVE   To engage participants in preparing a **problem statement**

TIME   Approximately 20 minutes

MATERIALS   Flip chart and marking pens

MINILECTURE   *The problem with problem solving is this, at least as far as G. K. Chesterton is concerned, "It isn't that they can't see the solution. It is that they can't see the problem." One technique that helps teams define their problem clearly is to have each team member work independently to define the problem (in writing) as he or she sees it. Members then share their definitions and work together until they have achieved a single problem statement that all members can agree on.*

Ideally, the team also writes—first individually and then collectively—an ideal state solution to the problem. In other words, what is the outcome members believe they are, or should be, working toward?

STEPS TO FOLLOW
1. Divide the class into teams of eight or nine.
2. Each team brainstorms a list of about 20 titles—of books, popular songs, movies, plays, ballets, operas, television programs, poems, etc. They work quickly to find one item on the list with which every member is familiar.
3. They define, alone and then together, the central problem of the selected item, using the approach described in the minilecture.

DISCUSSION QUESTIONS
- ✓ Can you think of a time when a problem was incorrectly defined and therefore an inappropriate solution found?
- ✓ Describe the gap between the real and the ideal in your work unit.
- ✓ Think of a work-related problem and define what it is and is *not*.

GAME STRETCHER   (5–60 minutes) Analyze actual workplace problems (from as many participants as possible) using this technique.

73

WEIGHTED VOTING

OBJECTIVE To provide experience with **weighted voting**

TIME Approximately 25 minutes

MATERIALS 3 ∞ 5 cards (one for each participant); flip chart and marking pens; Handout 73-1: Observer's Form

MINILECTURE *Francis Bacon referred to voting as voices "numbered and not weighed." But votes can be weighed and can prove valuable to team members as they move toward consensus. The weighted votes technique is especially useful when the number of possible choices is limited. Typically, the weighted voting technique proves most valuable when the team is trying to isolate and define the actual problem and later when the team is trying to select the best course of action.*

STEPS TO FOLLOW

1. Divide the class into teams of six participants, and ask one person to serve as leader. [*Note:* If five or fewer people are left over, they can serve as team observers and can use the Handout 73-1.]

2. Give each person a 3 ∞ 5 card and ask him/her to briefly describe a workplace problem. Collect the cards, shuffle them, and then give one problem (written on a card) to each team.

3. Have the team generate on chart paper four to six possible solutions to the problem.

4. On another sheet of chart paper, the teams will draw a grid. Vertically, on the left side, are written the names of the team members. Along the top are written the four to six choices. Each member is given a number of votes. [*Note:* The number is usually one and a half times the number of choices. So four choices give each member six votes, five yields seven votes, and six choices allows nine votes for each member.]

   Have members jot down their votes on paper before the tallying begins, and encourage them to spread their votes among the choices rather than allocate the total of nine "weights" to one choice. (If someone feels very strongly about a choice, he/she, of course, can give all the votes to that one option.)

5. The leader begins by displaying his/her votes in the grid and then calls on each person to state the sequence of votes quickly. The leader records the votes on the grid. The votes are totaled and a brief discussion is held concerning the direction in which the team seems to be leaning.

6. Point out that this technique is useful—not so much for reaching a vote but for learning how members feel prior to the final voting.

DISCUSSION QUESTIONS

✓ What other voting techniques are you aware of and/or do you use?

✓ What can the team leader do if one member clings tenaciously to an idea?

✓ What disadvantages might there be to the weighted voting technique?

OBSERVER'S FORM

1. Were the directions clear? Did the leader restate what the team was expected to do?

_____

_____

_____

_____

_____

2. What problems, if any, did the team run into?

_____

_____

_____

_____

_____

3. How efficiently did the team use the allotted time?

_____

_____

_____

_____

_____

4. How well did the leader handle the recording of information?

_____

_____

_____

_____

_____

5. What advice would you give this team?

_____

_____

_____

_____

_____

74

VITAL CONSIDERATIONS

OBJECTIVE To encourage participants to **assess proposal ideas** via VITAL criteria

TIME Approximately 25 minutes

MATERIALS Transparency 74-1; Handout 74-1: VITAL Criteria; flip chart paper; marking pens

MINILECTURE *Ideas have been called "the great warriors of the world" by James Garfield. But we all know what happens to warriors who enter battle without a battle plan or without the proper armament. I'd like to share with you today a simple way to subject your ideas to a scrutiny that will ideally help you emerge victorious from the battles that lie before you.*

But first let me offer you a problem to sharpen your wits and to remind you of how much can be made from so little. Only 26 letters of the alphabet and yet hundreds of thousands of words are created by them. Only a handful of people on a team and yet so many ideas for them to propose. [Show Transparency 74-1 and allow a few minutes for them to solve it.] The pattern is that the first line contains only letters composed of straight lines, the second line has letters with a straight line and a curve, and the third line has only curved letters.

STEPS TO FOLLOW
1. When the class members' cerebral juices are flowing after doing the transparency problem, divide the class into teams of seven or eight and appoint a leader for each team.

2. Allow about 10 minutes for the teams to decide on a workable solution for *one* of these common workplace problems (participants may wish to select a work-related problem of their own):

    Poor communication

    Stress

    Credit not given to those who deserve it

    Lack of cooperation

    Lack of empowerment

    Apathy

3. Once they have a workable solution, distribute copies of Handout 74-1 and allow about 10 minutes for the teams to analyze their solution in light of the criteria presented.

4. Discuss the value of this kind of scrutiny and encourage participants to use the VITAL criteria to evaluate ideas when they return to work and to their teams.

✓ What input is currently sought to aid your team in refining its ideas?

✓ Are corporate values considered in the decisions your team makes? Explain.

✓ How does your team know it is on the right track?

✓ How can you prevent the idea assessment process from becoming overly critical?

Figure out the pattern and then write the remaining letters of the alphabet in the right place.

```
A       E F   H I    K L M N
   B   D     G     J
      C                      O
```

VITAL CRITERIA

Directions: Once you and your team have decided on a workable solution to a workplace problem, analyze your solution using the VITAL criteria. (*Note:* Not every question pertains to your classroom team, but every question pertains to your actual workplace team. Assume that you are at work now and not in a training program.)

Value How serious is this problem?

Is it aligned with corporate goals?

Would it appear on most employees' top ten list?

How valued would the solution be? Is one possible?

What value can each of us add to the process of solving the problem?

Investment What will it cost to find/apply a solution?

What is the likely payoff?

How does the payoff compare to the potential cost?

What resources will we need?

Time How long will it take to solve this problem?

How long will it take to implement the solution?

How much time can we spare?

How much do we have?

Assessment What data do we need to collect?

Whose approval will we need?

What/who determines success and/or failure?

Learning What special skills will we need to acquire?

Who might have valuable knowledge for us?

Who knows what on our team?

What knowledge is needed to solve this problem?

OVERVIEW:
TOOLS OF THE DIVERGENT APPROACH

Not all problems can be solved with the scientific approach. Some problems call for creative solutions rather than logical and linear ones. For years, scientists have known that the two halves of the brain perform different functions: one highly analytical the other highly innovative. The divergent approach depends on spontaneity of thought, the unleashing of bright ideas, the stimulation of atypical, irreverent, "outside the box" thinking.

Fear prevents innovative thought. Being different, we have learned since grade school, often invites ridicule or disfavor. As we mature, we come to realize that it is safer to conform than to risk exposing individuality. So we develop patterns of *convergent* thinking, we restrict our own perceptions, and we find assurance in the herd mentality.

While management gurus like Tom Peters have led the way in appreciating the nonconformists and mental mavericks among us, many old school managers operate with this maxim, "It's my way or the highway."

Regardless of old style or new style managers, team leaders can encourage the kind of creativity that leads to high-quality solutions, which in turn lead to cost and cycle time reductions. As Keki R. Bhote asserts, "Quality is the engine that drives a company to the bank." With such a metaphorical image firmly implanted in the team's collective thinking, team leaders can explore various problem areas in relation to the quality of both their project and the team meeting process. Improvements in both areas are needed to increase productivity and ultimately profitability.

The exploration of these related ideas can lead teams to the selection of solutions with the highest potential for payoff. For example, using the image of the engine, the team leader might ask, "What prevents some companies from making it all the way to the bank?" As opposed to statistical thinking, this kind of imagining often leads to valuable insights. The answer might be, "They lost their way." Questions might then be raised about the company's strategic plans. The answer might be, "They ran out of gas." The questions that next spring to mind are, "Do we have the resources to sustain us?" Metaphorical thinking is only one of the many divergent approaches teams use to solve problems.

75

THINKING OUTSIDE THE BOX

OBJECTIVE
To encourage **analytical thinking** and **teamwork**

TIME
Approximately 10 minutes

MATERIALS
Handout 75-1: Don't Mangle the Angle; five inexpensive prizes for the winning team

MINILECTURE
You have probably heard the popular saying about data collection, "Without backup data, you are just another person with an opinion." It is usually not difficult for teams to gather the data. Analyzing them, though, is another matter.

Today I'd like you to work in teams of five to analyze the problem on the handout. You will have exactly 10 minutes, and there will be prizes for the winning team. Think creatively. Remember what Tom Peters has to say about innovative thinking: "Imagination is the main source of value in the new economy."

[ANSWER: Seven (The number inside each shape represents the number of other shapes that touch it.)]

STEPS TO FOLLOW
1. Divide the class into teams of five.

2. Distribute copies of Handout 75-1: Don't Mangle the Angle!

3. Allow 10 minutes for completion. Award the prizes to the winning team. If there is no winning team, explain the answer to the group. Remind them that solutions seldom depend on black-or-white alternatives. Successful problem solving usually requires the exploration of numerous possibilities.

DISCUSSION QUESTIONS
✓ What factors accounted for each team's success (or lack of success) in solving the problem?

✓ How did leadership in the team emerge?

✓ What alternative answers did the team explore?

✓ What caused or prevented the team members to think outside the box?

✓ What causes or prevents employees to think outside the box as they work to solve organizational problems?

✓ What kind of atmosphere is best for innovation?

✓ How can we create that atmosphere where we work?

GAME STRETCHER
(5–15 minutes) Ask the class if they have similar brain teasers. Allow time to work on a few and discuss afterwards the outside-the-box thinking that the solution requires.

DON'T MANGLE THE ANGLE

Problem: What number belongs in the shaded area?

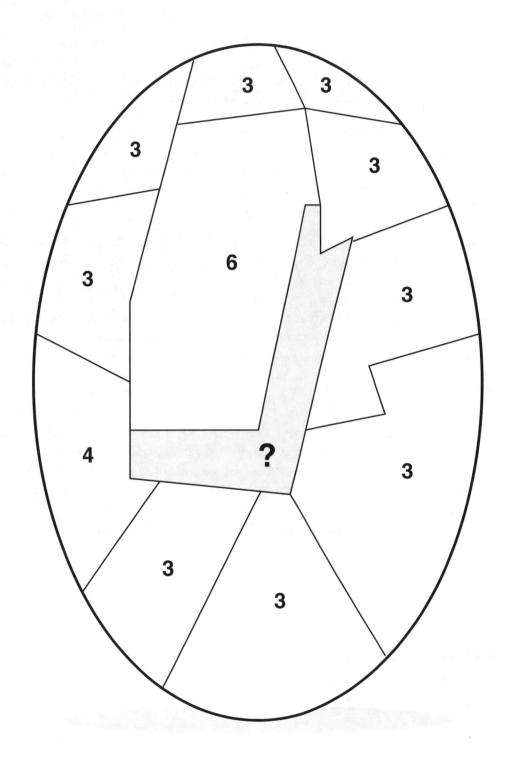

76

PUT OUT FOR OUTPUT!

OBJECTIVE   To encourage deliberative thought rather than wild speculation as an illustration of the need to **do it right the first time**

TIME   Approximately 15 minutes

MATERIALS   Handout 76-1: Output Oddity (One problem strip for each participant. This requires making enough copies of Handout 76-1 for one-fourth the class, then cutting the copies into four strips); Transparency 76-1

MINILECTURE   *Very often a problem seems easy to solve at first glance. But when we take the time for deeper investigation, we learn it isn't as easy as it may appear. One technique for solving complex problems is shared by Ray Kroc: "Nothing is particularly hard if you divide it into small jobs." When teams analyze an effect and its possible causes, they must make certain to probe deeply, to consider each possible contributing factor, to break the problem into many small sections. Jumping at what is obvious or superficial can lead us into hot water.*

STEPS TO FOLLOW
1. Divide the class into halves. Distribute the Output Oddity problem—one strip per participant. [*ANSWER: 15 lines, as shown on Transparency 76-1*]

2. Advise the teams they each have 15 minutes to solve the problem. The conditions are these: Team 1 cannot use paper or pencil but they *can* have five chances to declare their answer. (If the first answer is not correct, advise them of that and then permit them to have four other chances to supply the right answer.)

    Team 2 has only one chance to give you the right answer. However, they are allowed to use paper and pencil to determine their answer.

3. The teams should shout out the answer as soon as they have it.

4. When the 15-minute period has elapsed, show Transparency 76-1 and lead a discussion with these questions.

DISCUSSION QUESTIONS
✓ How well did your team do? What factors might explain your success or failure?

✓ Did anyone on the team have mathematical expertise? If so, was it used to solve the problem?

✓ Did team 2 try to solve the problem by drawing it? If so, did their graphic resemble Transparency 76-1?

✓ Can you think of instances when your organization, community (or even our nation) jumped at an easy solution instead of taking the time to study the problem in depth?

O U T P U T   ODDITY

Problem: There are six letters in the word *output*. How many lines must be drawn to connect each letter of the word to each of the other letters in the word?

O U T P U T   ODDITY

Problem: There are six letters in the word *output*. How many lines must be drawn to connect each letter of the word to each of the other letters in the word?

O U T P U T   ODDITY

Problem: There are six letters in the word *output*. How many lines must be drawn to connect each letter of the word to each of the other letters in the word?

O U T P U T   ODDITY

Problem: There are six letters in the word *output*. How many lines must be drawn to connect each letter of the word to each of the other letters in the word?

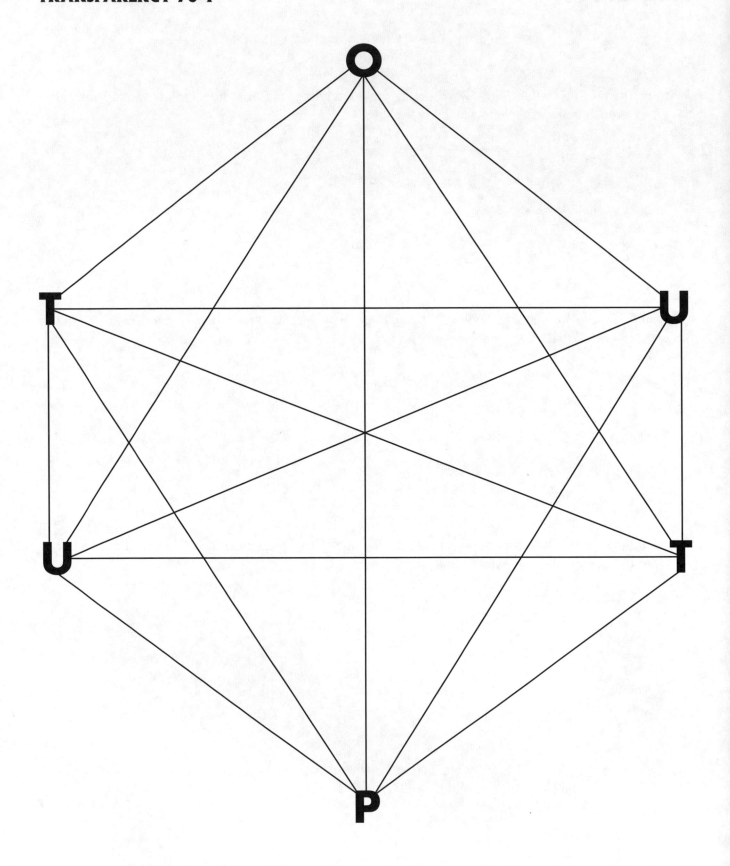

77

PROCESSES FROM A NEW PERSPECTIVE

OBJECTIVE	To promote **continuous improvement** via examination of familiar aspects of the work environment from various perspectives
TIME	Approximately 15 minutes
MATERIALS	Transparencies 77-1 and 77-2: Discussion Questions
MINILECTURE	*"Discovery," Albert Szent-Gyorgyi tells us, "consists of looking at the same thing as everyone else and thinking something different." Today, I'm going to show you part of a familiar, everyday word. However, because parts of the letters have been taken away, the word no longer looks familiar. Add three lines and it looks familiar again.*
	Once someone figures out what this word is, we will talk about ways to examine our work processes from an unusual perspective. We'll consider discovering a new or refined way to do the work. [Show Transparency 77-1.] *What is this word?* [Pause.] *Having a hard time? Okay, here's a clue: the word refers to a traveling person.* [Pause.] *Still having a hard time? Remember, you just have to add three lines.* [Note: The answer is HOBO.]

STEPS TO FOLLOW

1. Allow time for them to figure out the word. [If no one does, give them the answer. Add three lines to the numbers on Transparency 77-1 to create the word *HOBO*.]

2. Assuming someone figures out the answer, ask, "Did the answer just pop into your head or did you use a logical method to figure it out? [Many problem solvers will just stare at the word, waiting for the Muse to offer an answer. Others will realize the *3* is half of a *B*. From there, the answer comes easily.]

3. If it "popped," we are looking at the miracle and the mystery of creativity. If it was analyzed, however, ask the individual what technique he/she applied.

4. Continue with the minilecture.

MINILECTURE (continued)	*Sometimes we need to look at everyday practices from a new angle. We need to step back and examine component parts of a process to see if it can be improved or perhaps replaced altogether.*
	I'd like you to work with a partner now. Describe one of your work processes to him/her. Your partner tries to get you to look at your usual work in

an unusual way. Your partner helps you discover a new insight or element of the process. With questions like these, which your partner asks, we can work to "continuously improve." [Show Transparency 77-2.] Your partner's task is to get you to view a work process in a new way.

DISCUSSION QUESTIONS

✓ How does your process start?

✓ What do you do next? Next? Next?

✓ How does the process end?

✓ Why do you have to do that step?

✓ What parts of the process do not add value?

✓ What parts could be eliminated or combined?

✓ Where does this process waste time?

✓ What do customers complain about as far as the output is concerned?

✓ If you could design the process yourself, how would it differ from the current process?

STEPS TO FOLLOW (continued) **5.** Divide class into dyads and have them explore a process together.

GAME STRETCHER (15 minutes) Reverse roles. The original questioner can become the questioned. This time around, have the questioned person flowchart his/her process and then have the questioner ask about the diagram.

1   0   3   0

DISCUSSION QUESTIONS

How does your process start?

What do you do next? Next? Next?

How does the process end?

Why do you have to do that step?

What parts of the process do not add value?

What parts could be eliminated or combined?

Where does this process waste time?

What do customers complain about (in terms of the output)?

If you could design the process yourself, how would it differ from the current process?

SECTION 10
CONTINUOUS LEARNING

Do you work in an organizational Jurassic Park—a place with prehistoric mental monsters terrorizing those who try to bring them into the 20th century? Managers who rely on what has always worked for them (and it's logical to do so) find change upsetting. They cling, understandably, to what is familiar, what is comfortable, and what is sure to spell career suicide in time.

For example, those who refuse to learn to learn a computer because they are more comfortable with a typewriter soon find that the world cannot wait for them to catch up. Being caught up means paying daily attention to what is happening in the world of computers—or in any other world.

In this section, participants work on activities designed to broaden their thinking about how they think, how they work, and how they interact with others.

OVERVIEW: SHIFTING PARADIGMS

Emerson noted more than one hundred years ago that "a foolish consistency is the hobgoblin of little minds." More recently, Jack Welch of General Electric noted that if the rate of change outside the organization is greater than the rate of change inside, the organization is heading for trouble. Because technology impacts the marketplace so rapidly and societal shifts are occurring with such unprecedented speed, we are in a virtual adapt-or-die state.

Shifting one's world view, asking probing questions about the nature of employment, rethinking the organization and its structure, and more—all of this is required to remain competitive. The Frederick Taylor model of workers as hired hands—although not yet extinct—is quickly being replaced by a model that solicits and respects workers' ideas.

The nature of the workforce is changing. So, too, are the nature of the workplace and the work itself. The management style that may have been successful for the last 20 years is due for an overhaul.

We see the shift from managers managing their work units independently to a style fostered by partnerships and by an awareness of supplier-customer relationships. Rather than organizational isolates with connections primarily to their own managers, contemporary managers understand and work actively to expand their intra- and extraorganizational networks. There is a new sense of interdependency among managers and those they manage. In keeping with this new spirit is a shift from competition to cooperation, with input actively sought from internal and external sources.

Once content with a controlled environment, managers are now adapting to a more fluid set of circumstances that are more guided than directed to allow for the spontaneous combustion of good ideas.

78

HALF THE EQUATION

OBJECTIVE

To have participants **shift paradigms** regarding the best way to enter a training session and then to consider how **workplace paradigms are shifting**

TIME

Approximately 15 minutes

MATERIALS

Name card for each participant in a box (each name card has one of the following words on it). Thirty-two words are provided here; if there are more than 32 people, prepare extra name cards.

   bread, butter
   cause, effect
   peaches, cream
   bah, humbug
   frick, frack
   ham, eggs
   hill, dale
   rain, shine
   born, bred
   cut, dried
   milk, honey
   hello, good-bye
   David, Goliath
   Romeo, Juliet
   dollars, cents
   crime, punishment

STEPS TO FOLLOW

1. Mix the name cards up and give one to each participant as he/she enters the classroom. When everyone is present, ask them to find their partners by matching the words on their cards. For example, *bread* is a partner for *butter*. Once everyone is seated, begin the minilecture.

MINILECTURE

Typically, participants enter a classroom and make a beeline for their favorite seat—in the front, in the back, near the door, etc. When participants come to a session with a friend, they always [exaggerate the pronunciation of the word] sit with their friend. Today, I forced you to sit with someone else. You had to shift your paradigm and adjust to new circumstances. This simple exercise was probably accompanied by a mild degree of discomfort, unfamiliarity, perhaps even a slight anxiety as you left your usual pref-erences behind and participated in a new experience, with new rules and new players.

The exercise is a microcosmic example of the need to continuously learn, to go beyond stereotypical thinking, to experiment, and to reach out. The work-place is changing; the world is changing. We either drive the change or are dri-ven by it. Ideally, you can participate in the advances being made and the par-adigms being shifted.

In today's class, you will be exposed to new ideas. That's the whole point of taking a class. But if you discard those ideas because it's easier and more comfortable to think the thoughts you have always thought, then I will have failed you, you will have wasted a whole day of your life, and the organization will have wasted the money it spent to have you here.

Management guru Tom Peters tells employees, "If you have gone a whole week without being disobedient, you are doing yourself and your organization a disservice." This attitude, refreshing and useful though it is, is probably very dif-ferent from the attitude you were encouraged to have when you first entered the workforce. I'd like you to work with your partner now to contemplate some of the ways—attitudinal, technological, structural—that the workplace has changed since you first entered it.

STEPS TO FOLLOW (continued)

2. Ask the partners to prepare a list of at least 10 items that represent changes in the workplace from the time they first entered the workforce to the present.

3. Ask, "Did anyone here enter the work before 1980?" (Keep asking until you get the first year someone in the room entered the workforce.) Then point out that from that earliest year to the present, we have seen serious changes. Call on several pairs to share a few of their observations. Con-clude by pointing out that we have had to shift paradigms and that we will need to continue making such shifts.

DISCUSSION QUESTIONS

✓ How do you interpret Tom Peters' statement?

✓ What paradigms have you had to shift over the last five years?

✓ Knowing what you now know, what advice would you give to a young per-son just entering the workforce?

✓ How does that advice differ from the advice *you* were given?

GAME STRETCHER

(10 minutes) Ask the pairs to review their list and to prepare a one-sentence re-sponse to this prompt: "What does it all mean?" (Or, "What does it all portend for the future?")

79

DINOSAUR BRAINS

OBJECTIVE   To encourage use of analogy to describe **change in the organizational culture**

TIME   Approximately 15 minutes

MATERIALS   Handout 79-1: Dinosaur Brains

MINILECTURE   *It's impossible to stop change. Yet many people exert considerable energy trying to do just that. The changes may require physical or mental adaptation but if we do not adapt, we are doomed to extinction, much like the dinosaur. The popular phrase "dinosaur brains" is an analogy referring to the mindset of people who are mired in the practices of the past. They are either unaware of current forces or unwilling to incorporate those forces into their daily practices.*

Think about your own practices and those of your manager. Are they up to date? Or are they rooted in the past and difficult to shift? How would your co-workers describe your practices? Making a comparison or using an analogy such as "dinosaur brains" often helps us see ourselves and our behavior in a new light. As G. Polya, a Stanford University mathematician noted, "All sorts of analogy may play a role in the discovery of the solution and so we should not neglect any sort."

STEPS TO FOLLOW

1. Distribute Handout 79-1 and allow about 10 minutes for participants to complete it.

2. Form small groups of three and ask them to share their worksheet responses with one another. *Warning:* Reinforce the fact that they need not reveal whether their descriptions refer to their bosses or to themselves.

DISCUSSION QUESTIONS

✓ How is it possible for past successes to lead to subsequent failures?

✓ What external forces require paradigm shifts?

✓ As a nation, what paradigm shifts have we undergone?

✓ What causes people to cling to what they know rather than embrace what they do not yet know?

DINOSAUR BRAINS

Directions: Select any one of the following figures and use it to describe your basic mindset or paradigm as far as change is concerned. To which animal would you compare your thinking and why? If you prefer, you can describe your *manager's* basic mindset toward change. (You need not reveal which mindset you are describing—yours or the boss's.)

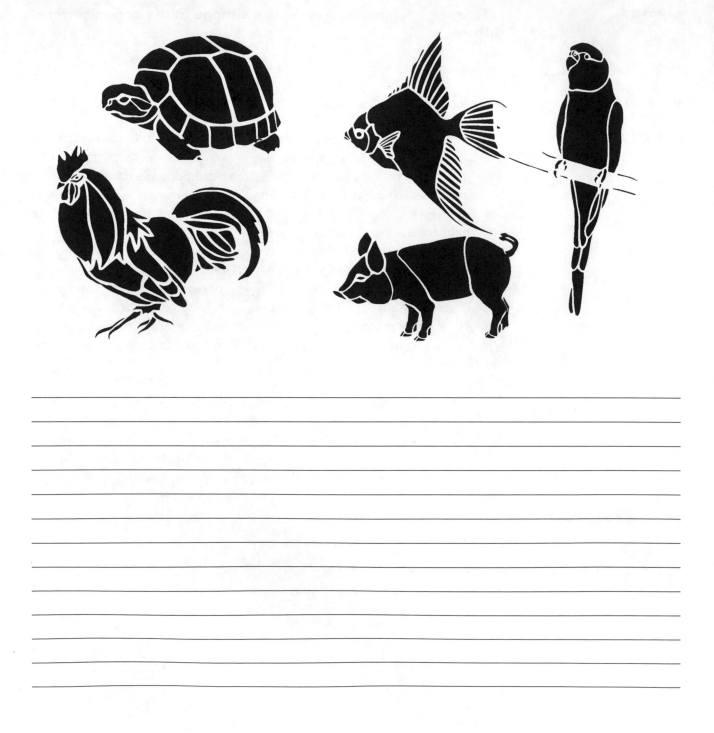

_____

_____

_____

_____

_____

_____

_____

_____

_____

_____

_____

_____

80

BREAK DOWN OR BREAK THROUGH?

OBJECTIVE   To encourage **receptivity to change** by illustrating that when change is gradual, the results are often greater than when change is imposed as a dramatic breakthrough

TIME   Approximately 5 minutes

MATERIALS   Pennies—one for each class participant; Transparency 80-1

MINILECTURE   *"Kaizen" is a Japanese word that means gradual, incremental change as opposed to dramatic breakthrough. While pronounced change carries with it pronounced impact in the way things are done, efficiency may suffer as a result. Breaking down the components of the change to be implemented may yield better results than attempting to implement the change in one fell swoop.*

As H. L. Mencken observed, "For every complex problem, there is one solution that is simple, neat and wrong." Rather than solve problems by grasping the first solution to appear, teams should examine thoroughly, gradually, perhaps even incrementally. Breakthroughs and "Eureka" solutions do occur and do have value. However, for the majority of problems—and the changes their solutions create—the gradual approach is usually more meaningful and more readily accepted.

Let me illustrate this concept for you if I might. Let's assume that I were willing to give you a sum of money each day for one entire month. Would you rather have $1000 each day for 31 days or would you rather have a penny on the first day and a doubled amount for the next thirty days? [Call on a few people to share their thoughts.]

Well, let me begin the process for you. [Distribute one coin to each person.] *Here is your penny for day one. Begin to calculate now.* [Allow time for calculations.] *Now that you have doubled the amount for 30 days, would you still wish to have $1000 for 31 consecutive days?*

Sometimes we leap at solutions that initially seem quite attractive. After careful analysis, though, these glittering prospects often pale in comparison to solutions carefully and deliberately wrought. Organizational leaders, believing that their new system or procedure or philosophy is indeed attractive, sometimes attempt to impose it all at once upon employees. A gradual introduction, while it may take longer to implement, is usually more successful in the long run. Similarly, problems that are probed and scrutinized from multiple perspectives yield solutions that cannot come about by quick response.

1. After participants are through with their calculations, show Transparency 80-1 to ensure they correctly calculated. Point out that, at first blush, $31,000 is truly an appealing sum—especially compared to a paltry penny. But the effect of doubling is so much greater than could be imagined. Stress again the significance of the Mencken quotation.

2. Lead a brief discussion about the fact that as leaders, they are change agents. For most people, gradually-introduced change is easier to accept than dramatic change. The end result, however, is usually more warmly embraced due to thorough understanding/acceptance along the way.

DISCUSSION QUESTIONS

✓ Think of a change that has recently come about in your (business) life. Was it introduced gradually or dramatically? How well did you cope with the change?

✓ What progress has your team or work unit made lately? What change accompanied that progress?

✓ About what have you changed your mind in the last five years?

✓ Can you think of a leader—organizational or otherwise—who has *not* effected change?

✓ What can the organization do to reassure people about change?

PENNY POWER

1.	.01	**16.**	327.68
2.	.02	**17.**	655.36
3.	.04	**18.**	1,310.72
4.	.08	**19.**	2,621.44
5.	.16	**20.**	5,242.88
6.	.32	**21.**	10,485.76
7.	.64	**22.**	20,971.52
8.	1.28	**23.**	41,943.04
9.	2.56	**24.**	83,886.08
10.	5.12	**25.**	167,772.16
11.	10.24	**26.**	335,544.32
12.	20.48	**27.**	671,088.64
13.	40.96	**28.**	1,342,177.20
14.	81.92	**29.**	2,684,354.40
15.	163.84	**30.**	5,368,708.80
		31.	10,737,417.60

OVERVIEW: SHIFTING ROLES

Today's workers have the chance to expand their roles in ways that would have raised eyebrows, if not hackles, 10 years ago. The Quality movement has inverted pyramids. This means ordinary employees are now involved in making decisions, solving problems, improving processes—activities that years ago would have remained the exclusive domain of managers. In many companies, employees *own* the company and so they have to engage in managerial functions.

Today's employees have unlimited opportunities to serve on teams, to lead teams, to develop managerial and leadership skills, to be empowered—whether or not they have any inclination to become managers. Being empowered means shifting the way roles have traditionally been defined. It means accepting the multidimensional composite the workforce requires in each of its employees.

That composite expects that all workers—knowledge workers and others—will become knowledge seekers. Since a basic precept of quality requires an understanding of our dependence on suppliers to provide the inputs that begin our work processes, we need to exchange information with the suppliers regarding our standards. Therfore, quality in means quality out. At the end of the work process is the customer, who regards employes as suppliers. Again, the more knowledge we have of customers' needs, the better we are able to supply the quality they need.

Continuous improvement means continuous learning about ways to raise the bar of excellence. To stagnate mentally about products/processes/services is to do the organization a disservice.

Employees in Quality-driven organizations actively seek training. They want more and better tools—and not just the physical kind—for work that in itself is in a constant, if gradual, state of flux. They have obligations too to share their knowledge. Flowcharting, for example, enables employees to scrutinize existing processes and to show others how the work flows.

81

FROM IRON TO LEAD(ER)

OBJECTIVE   To promote consideration of emerging shifts in the **manager's role**

TIME   Approximately 10 minutes

MATERIALS   Transparencies 81-1, 81-2, and 81-3; token prize

MINILECTURE   *Lawrence Holpp strongly asserts that organizations today are beginning to acknowledge that they have only two choices as far as managers are concerned: "Either they must develop a new role for supervisors in managing the quality-improvement activities of various groups of people, or they must abandon the traditional role of supervisory entirely and move toward semi-autonomous teams."*

Yesterday's leaders were iron-fisted, heavy-handed in their dealings with subordinates. Today's leaders are more like coaches, usually serving the teams rather than controlling them. For some supervisors, the change from autocrat to coach has been natural; for others, it has been impossible.

As human beings, we are capable of change, sometimes radical change. To illustrate this, I'd like you to look at this transparency. [Show Transparency 81-1.] Note that each word resembles the word in front of it except that one letter has been changed.

Next, I'd like you to see if you can move from "iron" to "lead" with just six words between. The letters do not have to remain in the same order, but only one of them can be changed. [Show Transparency 81-2.]

[If someone figures out the problem, show Transparency 81-3 and award the prize. If no one figures it out, simply show the answer on 81-3.]

STEPS TO FOLLOW   **1.** Divide the team in pairs. Show the first transparency, and answer any questions about how to get from the first word to the last.

2. Show the second and the third transparencies. Then move into the discussion questions.

DISCUSSION QUESTIONS   ✓ Do you agree with Holpp's statement? Why or why not?

✓ Who manages the quality improvement activities in your firm?

✓ What would happen in your organization if the traditional role of supervisor were entirely abandoned?

✓ What expectations might be associated with a new role for supervisors?

✓ What is your definition of a semiautonomous team?

✓ Would you like to work on such a team? Explain.

GAME STRETCHER (10 minutes) Have teams of four list ways that supervisors in today's workplace play a role that is different from the role they were expected to play 20 years ago.

HEAD
HEAL
TEAL
TELL
TALL
TAIL

IRON

— — — —

— — — —

— — — —

— — — —

— — — —

— — — —

LEAD

IRON

ICON

COIN

CORN

CORD

LORD

LOAD

LEAD

82

MULTIPLE ROLES

OBJECTIVE

To encourage participants to recognize the **multiple roles each employee is able to play**

TIME

Approximately 15 minutes

MATERIALS

Transparency 82-1

MINILECTURE

President George Bush once remarked that "the definition of a successful life must include service to others." Each of us has numerous examples of how we serve others, but within the work environment we tend to restrict the number of roles we play, and the number of ways we can serve others. It may be that our job descriptions limit us. Perhaps we limit ourselves by not experimenting with our capacities. Perhaps our managers limit us by not giving us challenging tasks.

I, for example, in addition to being a trainer, am sometimes called on to perform as a magician. In a sense, I "serve" as an entertainer for patients in nursing homes or children in hospitals. You don't believe me? Well, let me get a volunteer from the audience and I'll show you.

STEPS TO FOLLOW

1. Find the volunteer and ask him or her to think of a one-digit or two-digit number. Ask him/her to:

> Double the number.
>
> Add 12.
>
> Divide the total by two.
>
> Subtract the original number.

When he/she has completed the calculations, say, "Is the remainder 6?" [It always is.]

2. Share the fact that you've enjoyed this other role and that it has not been that difficult to learn your magic tricks.

3. Showing Transparency 82-1, have each person select a partner. Each person selects two roles that he/she plays in the workplace, roles that directly or indirectly serve others. The person briefly tells the partner how he/she plays these roles. Then, the speaker becomes the listener as the *other* person explains the two roles he/she has selected.

DISCUSSION QUESTIONS

✓ Scientists tell us that we are only using about one-tenth of our intellectual power. What things have you not yet done that you believe you are capable of doing?

✓ America has sometimes been criticized as a nation that hires its workforce for their hands and not for their heads. How would you respond to that charge?

✓ Some organizations hold job switch days, to deepen employees' appreciation of the daily difficulties faced and overcome by their co-workers. How would you go about instituting such an event in your organization?

✓ Research tells us that a competent secretary can handle 90 percent of the phone calls that come in to her boss's office each day. What percentage of your boss's work do you think you could handle? What percentage would you *like* to handle?

GAME STRETCHER

(20 minutes) Form groups of 10 and have participants role play a meeting. They assume one of the roles on Transparency 82-1. One possible meeting topic is, "How can the organization learn about and then use the dormant capacities of the workforce?" During the meeting, they can brainstorm a list of 15 to 20 ideas and then select the most workable one.

Magician	Teacher
Advocate	Inventor
Psychologist	Priest
Host(ess)	Gambler
Storyteller	Doctor
Social worker	Cop
Energizer	Leader
Manager	Follower
Catalyst	Rebel
Editor	Director
Builder	Surgeon
Entrepreneur	Judge

OVERVIEW: SHIFTING RESPONSIBILITIES

When paradigms shift to recognize the greater contribution that each of us can make, when roles expand to tap latent potential, newly empowered employees assume a corresponding shift in their responsibilities. As employees work to improve processes, they eliminate nonvalue-added steps, thereby allowing time for other tasks to be done. As they gain empowerment, they simultaneously reduce their dependence on multiple levels of management.

Restaurant servers who are empowered to take 25 percent off the bill of a dissatisfied customer without first asking the boss's permission are functioning as managers. They're required to think like managers instead of solely like servers. In an instant, they must decide if their action is fair, precedent-setting, too generous, or not generous enough. They must weigh the loss to the restaurant against the possible loss of a customer. They must think about how often they make such overtures and whether their decisions are impacting the bottom line.

In many ways, it is easier to remain unempowered than to assume the additional responsibilities required of those in traditional management or leadership roles. Quality (with all its tenets) may be free, as Philip Crosby asserts, but it is never easy.

Employees feel uneasy as they shift their paradigms, their roles, their responsibilities. But accompanying the unease is a sense of challenge, which in time overwhelms the discomfort and leads employees to seek further changes. Proactivity is expected of employees in organizations obsessed with quality, as are teamwork and involvement. For most employees, these new expectations cause some mental discomfort—but only temporarily.

83

PROJECTING "MANAGEMENT"

OBJECTIVE

To give participants experience with basic **project management** requirements

TIME

Approximately 30 minutes

MATERIALS

Transparency 83-1: Project Management Guidelines; chart paper; marking pens; masking tape or push pins; Handout 83-1: Observer's Form (3 copies)

MINILECTURE

You may have the opportunity to work as a manager before you retire. Perhaps you will have the official title of manger or the less permanent title of project manager. You may be responsible for managing a number of things, including the special talents of your team. Keep in mind what Virgil had to say: "We are all not capable of everything." Break the project into tasks and delegate responsibility for the tasks to the talented people working with you and for you.

Today several of you will have an opportunity to serve as managers of a very short project. Here are the guidelines you should follow as you work on this project and on future projects. [Show transparency.]

STEPS TO FOLLOW

1. Choose three people to be the project administrators. (These three also serve as observers; so give each of them the Observer's Form.) If possible set them up at a table away from the working teams.

2. Divide the remaining class members into teams of eight or nine. Appoint a leader for each and distribute chart paper, pens, and masking tape or push pins.

3. Give all the teams the same project: They are to prepare, in a 20-minute period, a microlist of their individual responsibilities and from that, develop a three- or four-item macrolist. The macrolist is to have umbrella terms—large categories in which several of the individual responsibilities can be clustered. The word *miscellaneous* as a category is not permitted.

   There should also be a short written explanation of the project to package the umbrella terms. In other words, their final product should not simply have three terms plopped on the chart paper. There should be at least one sentence to introduce or explain the macroterms and at least one sentence to finish off the written presentation.

4. Explain that, before the project can be deemed successful, it must meet the approval of the project administrators, people who typically assist teams prior to the approval-granting stage. Point out that three project administra-

tors are sitting in the back of the room. [*Note:* Upon completion of the exercise, only the teams that sought and obtained approval from the administrators will be declared successful.]

5. After 20 minutes, announce that time is up and have the project administrators share their observations with the class.

✓ Projects have a life cycle. What are the stages in this cycle? [*Note:* Answers will vary, but typically there are four C's: Concept stage, Consolidation stage, Conduct stage, and Completion stage.]

✓ What activities would you list in each stage?

✓ What resources are available in your organization to assist at each stage?

✓ What characteristics does an effective project manager possess?

✓ How does project management differ from regular management?

PROJECT MANAGEMENT GUIDELINES

1. Make others aware of the goal. Check for understanding.

2. Ask for assistance inside and outside the team.

3. Establish a time line.

4. Give status report to administrators and gain approval **before** reaching the end of the project.

OBSERVER'S FORM

1. If the leader (or a delegate) asks for assistance, give him/her one of the three macroterms that describe many responsibilities: transforming information. If asked for further assistance, you are free to give the opening sentences for their report: "Today's employee is tasked with a great many responsibilities. Generally speaking, though, those responsibilities can be clustered around three broad terms."

The overhead and the instructor both encouraged the teams to turn to you for assistance. Did they? Why or why not? _____

_____
_____
_____
_____
_____

2. Again, teams were asked twice to seek your approval before their project could reach a successful conclusion. Did they ask for that approval? Why or why not ? _____

_____
_____
_____
_____
_____

3. What did the leaders do to ensure everyone understood the task? Did the leaders check with the administrators at any time to make sure they were doing the right thing?_____

_____
_____
_____
_____
_____

4. How effectively did the leaders break down the task and delegate responsibilities?

_____
_____
_____
_____
_____

5. Did the leaders establish time lines and work to ensure that they were met? Explain.

_____
_____
_____
_____
_____

84

FAST OR SLOW, BUT ALWAYS ACCURATE

OBJECTIVE To help participants assess existing skills and to encourage the **development of new skills**

TIME Approximately 10 minutes

MATERIALS Handout 84-1: Accurate Action; watch or clock with a second hand; flip chart; marking pen

MINILECTURE *"Skill to do," Ralph Waldo Emerson maintained, "comes of doing." We all possess skills. If our desire to increase the number of our skills is strong enough, we begin practicing new ones. In time, our clumsy overtures become polished skills. The broader the range of skills, of course, the more marketable we are. The more we learn how to do, the more valuable we become in terms of employment.*

I have a short exercise for you. It will assess your skill at doing a particular kind of work. No matter which way you are assessed, remember there is work that calls for that particular assessed skill. If you wish to develop other skills, all you need is practice.

If you finish the assessment ahead of others, note the time, and then go back to check your work.

STEPS TO FOLLOW

1. Distribute Handout 84-1 and go over the directions with participants. Then ask if everyone understands what has to be done. Write the starting time on the flip chart or whiteboard.

2. After two minutes, say, "Stop" and move to the discussion questions. Remind participants that this simple test is only a 2-minute assessment. As such, it should not be relied on exclusively as an indicator of their skills. However, if the results after 20 different tests are the same, they can be fairly certain that the indication is correct. Stress again that we need both types of people—fast/accurate and slow/accurate in the workplace. If they were fast/inaccurate or slow/inaccurate, they will need to develop their accuracy skills.

DISCUSSION QUESTIONS

✓ What kind of work do we expect fast/accurates to do? [*Note:* Typically, we need fast/accurates to do work that requires moving and thinking quickly.]

✓ Think of fast/accurates you know. How would you describe them? What does their work require of them?

✓ What kind of work do we depend on slow/accurates to do? [*Note:* Typically, we need slow/accurates to do detailed work that requires careful attention and persistence.]

- ✓ Think of slow/accurates you know. How would you describe them? What kind of work do they do?
- ✓ If your job changed and your new job required the opposite skills, how easily could you meet the new requirement?

GAME STRETCHER

(5 minutes) Such exercises are fairly easy to prepare. You may wish to have others available for those seeking to add another kind of skill to the ones they already possess.

ACCURATE ACTION

Directions: For this exercise, you have exactly two minutes. Accuracy is what we are after here, so work as accurately as you can and as quickly as you can. Your task is to draw a line through all the *numbers* you can find in the lines below. (Count capital O's as zeroes.)

JKL7NP1P9P3PXP2P54PGP6JW2QNY1V9UP8VZ2MTBNU16V9N73JGH8B62T

MAY4DF6Q1GD8V6EW4B8V3K2K5N6N8NE3NSO1CV9RTNY2NF4IV7QBLFD8

NO5AG3SD5F6JH7PHOI9SD2CNCK4L3HVUS9R4KN8SG2VDLG843GAQKD7FG3

4HFGSDGGF9S7GF6S5F4A4FD4V6H7RT9405JDH7DS6QG3G5IUG87S6DGH4U3

9GJH4NDF8XH45B3DG2QK5EIU0A3MGAODH2N1D07BB532H2M3SGJD8CW35

S5LX1CH4BV7VKE7V2GB6QU5OL3EJ3KSD0F2GJ9JK1H3FDJLO3E98Y2JH45D1

KJF3LKJR4SDFLKJ8V93K5620TK2LKN5609CJ234KJGHC86124JHJKFDV98213

When the instructor announces that time is up, exchange your paper with a partner. The partner checks to see whether you missed any numbers on your paper and whether you crossed out any that were letters instead of numbers. You check your partner's paper, looking for the same errors.

If you *finished* the test in two minutes or less *and* had three errors or less, you can consider yourself a fast/accurate. If you did not finish the test but had three errors or less, you are probably a slow/accurate. If you finished but had more than three errors, you are probably fast/inaccurate. If you did not finish but had more than three errors, you are probably slow/inaccurate. If you fall into the latter two categories, work to build both your speed and accuracy.

85

SYSTEMS THINKING

OBJECTIVE	To promote systems thinking
TIME	Approximately 15 minutes
MATERIALS	Transparency 85-1: Circle of Influence

MINILECTURE

"The key to seeing reality systemically," Peter Senge declares, *"is seeing circles of influence rather than straight lines."* Systems thinking encourages us to see the big picture, rather than merely our small place in it. Equipped with an understanding of the system itself, we can develop a better understanding of our contribution to it.

Look at the transparency. [Show Transparency 85-1.] It depicts the impact of one department's action on other departments. In this case, the five functional areas are Operations, Engineering, Marketing, Administration, and Sales and Distribution.

Administration receives a letter from a customer, complaining about a potential danger in the product. Administration directs Engineering to correct the problem. Engineering passes blueprints for the revised product to Operations, who, in turn, shares the prototype with Marketing. Marketing shares their new advertising campaign with the Sales Department. The sales figures for the new product are shared with Administration and a new cycle begins. (All this naturally occurs over a protracted period. Our microcosmic, individual actions have shorter, less wide-ranging impact.)

STEPS TO FOLLOW

1. Discuss the circle of influence.

2. Have participants work in pairs to draw similar circles depicting the impact that a singular action on their part might have on the actions of other functional areas.

3. Select two circle drawings and have the "owners" transfer their circles to chart paper while you engage the class in the discussion questions. Then have the two owners explain how their work actions impact other departments and other functional areas.

DISCUSSION QUESTIONS

✓ As you examined the system's circle of influence, what insights did you glean about who your customers are? Did you acquire any insights about why you do what you do?

✓ Why is it important for each employee to engage in systems thinking from time to time?

✓ What forces prevent us from engaging in this kind of thinking?

✓ If you could change the circle you have drawn to make it more efficient or less expensive, how would you redesign it?

(10 minutes) Have partners draw circles of influence for nonwork parts of their lives. For example, what might be the impacts of:

✓ A minister's Sunday sermon?

✓ A Little League team winning a championship?

✓ A supermarket announcing a $10 rebate on vegetables?

✓ A young man deciding to buy roses for his sweetheart (or vice versa)?

CIRCLE OF INFLUENCE

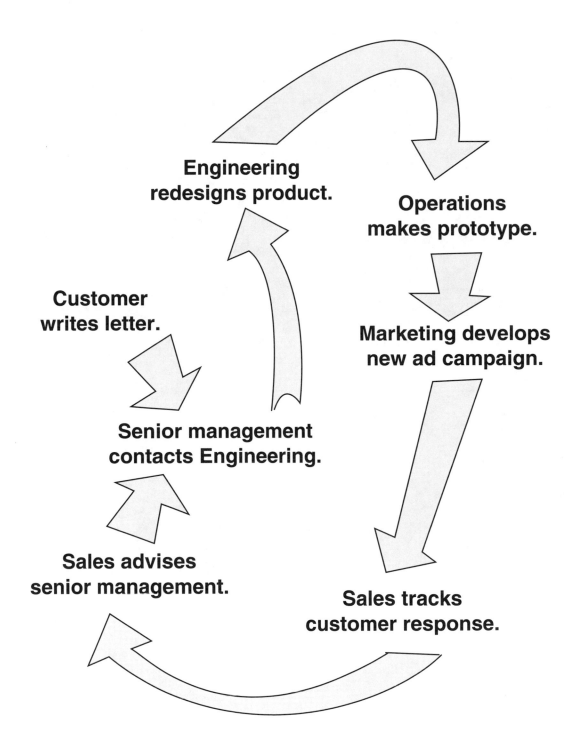

Engineering redesigns product.

Operations makes prototype.

Customer writes letter.

Marketing develops new ad campaign.

Senior management contacts Engineering.

Sales advises senior management.

Sales tracks customer response.

SECTION 11
BENCHMARKING

Benchmarking is not a new practice for those interested in the pursuit of excellence. Such individuals and organizations are already engaged—formally or informally—in the process of comparison, in order to appreciate their strengths and to strengthen their weaknesses.

The Quality movement, however, with its emphasis on bettering the best, has effected a benchmarking construct and a set of guidelines with which organizations can codify their efforts to become world-class competitors.

This section presents those guidelines and encourages their adaptation by organizations.

OVERVIEW: INTERNAL PARTNERS

Two people, working on the same process, may well perform the processes in two different ways. Each brings his/her experience to the work, and that experience influences how the work is done. The sequence of steps may vary slightly, or major differences may occur in the input *to* the process or in the output created *by* the process. But it is inaccurate to assume that 12 different people working on the same process are working in exactly the same way.

Through informal discussions in the workplace, we can compare how we do our work with how others do theirs. In this way, we learn of shortcuts or of ways to reduce the time or number of errors. We learn from others, and they from us. Through such comparisons, we form internal partnerships in the spirit of continuous improvement. The spirit, of course, can be extended to include those who do not perform the same work we do but whose work has a bearing on ours—at either the beginning or the end of a process.

One means of internal benchmarking is the self-audit, ideally conducted organizationwide. It calls for assessing current performance against jointly established goals or standards, such as those specified by authoritative bodies like the Malcolm Baldrige Award committee or the President's Quality Award examiners.

Processes that receive high marks are analyzed to discover how and why they are succeeding. The corresponding documentation permits replication of successful practices. Processes that receive low marks are also analyzed—to learn where and why they are failing.

Internal benchmarking is most effective when coupled with external benchmarking because internal benchmarking alone narrows our vision of excellence. Without the highest standards by which to gauge our excellence, we tend to think that what currently exists is best. The classic comparison of the optimist and the pessimist strikes a relevant chord: the optimist believes there is no place in the world better than this corporation. The pessimist believes the optimist is correct. Benchmarking will tell.

When we turn the quality spotlight only on ourselves, we can compare ourselves only to last year's results. Cognizant only of what has been done in the past, we limit the possibilities for the future.

86

WORKPLACE INTERDEPENDENCY

OBJECTIVE   To develop understanding of the **internal customer** concept

TIME   Approximately 10 minutes

MATERIALS   Small area rug such as a bathroom rug

MINILECTURE   *"Cooperation,"* Charles Steinmetz assures us, *"is not a sentiment—it is an economic necessity."* Employees sometimes become narrow in their thinking about their work, concentrating on what must be done without realizing for whom it is being done. Each of us serves as a link in a very large chain. The next link is the customer of our outputs, the employee who depends on our output in order to continue the next step in the macro process of providing goods or services to a paying customer. (The person who takes orders over the phone, for example, must contact the warehouse, which prepares the order for shipping.)

I have a game that demonstrates the importance of depending on one another to increase our productivity or efficiency. It shows how cooperation, with a little creativity, can help us exceed expectations.

Can you all see this rug? [Move it to the center area in the front of the room, or encourage participants to stand so that they can see it easily.] How many people do you think we can fit on this rug? They must stand on the rug—no parts of their bodies can touch the bare floor. [Elicit answers.] Well, let's have a few of you come up so we can try it out.

STEPS TO FOLLOW   **1.** Volunteers will probably need to make several attempts and may need to think through the process of squeezing bodies onto the rug, becoming more efficient each time they try. Encourage them to do better each time until they fit 20 bodies. If they all stand on just one foot and hold on to the other players, it is possible to get that many on it. Remind them that it takes interdependency and creative thinking to move beyond their initial expectations of success.

2. Point out that each of us is capable of greater productivity, efficiency, and creativity than we have yet experienced. But the greater results do not come about unless we are willing to explore our creative potential, willing to communicate, and work cooperatively with our internal customers and suppliers.

DISCUSSION QUESTIONS   ✓ How often do you ask for, or give your internal partners, information about what you need to do your job more efficiently?

✓ Think of a workplace process that you feel needs to be improved. Besides your department members, which internal customer and which internal supplier would be valuable additions to a team assembled to improve that process?

✓ What examples are there in your workplace of different departments working together to do something that has never been done before?

87

REMOVING BLINDERS

OBJECTIVE To encourage positive thinking about **workplace partnerships**

TIME Approximately 15 minutes

MATERIALS Handout 87-1: Paradigm Shifting for Problem Solving

MINILECTURE *An old French proverb warns that "to think a thing impossible is to make it so." We sometimes ascribe the word* impossible *to possible endeavors merely because we are used to doing what we've always done. Sometimes we declare impossibility because we lack the vision to go beyond the existing circumstances. Sometimes our paradigms are so deeply entrenched that we are not willing to exert the energy required to shift them. But those shifts are needed if we are to do things we've not done before, or to think things we've not thought before.*

Handout 87-1 contains puzzles and riddles that require you to move your mindset just a little to the left or a little to the right to consider the problem in a nontypical way. Until you do that, you probably will not be able to answer the questions correctly. Once you have finished the handout, do some mindset shifting in relation to your job.

STEPS TO FOLLOW **1.** Divide teams into dyads or triads, and distribute Handout 87-1. Allow about 5 minutes for completion.

2. Ask, "Does any pair think they have all the correct answers?" Call upon a spokesperson to share them. [The answers all require careful consideration of the words in the puzzle; they also require us not to jump to conclusions based on what we *think* we understand. It requires shifting mental mindsets to figure out the answers, which appear below.]

   1. The word *man* is what misleads us. The teams could have been composed of boys, girls, or women.

   2. It takes five engineers five minutes to sketch a prototype. This means that each engineer needs five minutes to draw one prototype. One engineer, then, could draw 12 sketches in one hour, and 100 engineers could sketch 1200 prototypes in one hour.

   3. Holes contain no dirt.

   4. He had three hours sleep: from 7 P.M. to 10 P.M.

   5. Volume II was in front of Volume I. To go from the last page of Volume II to the first page of Volume I requires the bookworm to go through two book covers and just two pages.

3. After explaining the answers, consider handout questions 6 and 7. Then proceed to the discussion questions.

✓ What words tend to force our thinking in one direction and keep it there, preventing us from looking at a situation from different angles?

✓ Other than words, what prevents us from giving full consideration to other people, other ideas, or other ways of doing things?

✓ Would you describe your current relationship with your boss as a partnership? If not, what could you do to make it so?

✓ What kind of partnerships would you like to form in the workplace? What might be the result of each of them?

HANDOUT 87-1

PARADIGM SHIFTING FOR PROBLEM SOLVING

Directions: Work with a partner to solve these five problems. (Make note of partnership behaviors.) When you have the answers, let the instructor know and then continue with the two questions at the end of this handout.

1. A baseball game went the full nine innings and the final score was 3 to 0—in favor of Katz's Cats. The spectators, who had applauded their respective teams, did not see a single man touch third base despite the score. How could this be? _____

2. If five engineers can sketch five prototypes in five minutes, how many prototypes can 100 engineers sketch in one hour? _____._____

3. How much dirt is there in a hole one foot deep, one foot long, and one foot wide? _____

4. Mr. Jones, Chief Financial Officer for a small manufacturing firm, got home at about 7 P.M. on a Friday afternoon, exhausted after a particularly grueling week. He told his family he wanted no dinner; he only wanted to sleep. And he promptly set his alarm for 10 A.M. the next morning. (As it was a Saturday, he knew he could sleep late.) Assuming he slept without interruption, how many hours of sleep did he have by the time the alarm went off? _____

5. Two manuals about ISO-9000 (quality documentation procedures) are sitting on a bookshelf in your office. A bookworm eats its way from page 1 of Volume I to the last page of Volume II. Each volume has 100 pages, and yet the worm only ate two covers and two pages. How is this possible? _____

6. Other than yourself, on whom do you depend to do the very best work of which you are capable? ___

7. What improvements might be effected if you formed a partnership with those who supply you with what you need to do your work, with the person who receives the work you do, and with one external customer? _____

88

CARPE—DON'T CARP—THE DIEM

OBJECTIVE To provide an opportunity for self-assessment as a prelude to initiating a **workplace partnership**

TIME Approximately 20 minutes

MATERIALS Transparency 88-1; Handout 88-1: Self-Assessment

MINILECTURE *"Small opportunities," Demosthenes commented, "are often the beginning of great enterprises." All around us are opportunities to improve the quality of our work. So why aren't more people seizing those opportunities? The answer usually lies with the fact that we do not take time (or feel we cannot take time) to think about ways we can join forces with others to optimize efforts.*

Today I'm going to give you time to fill out an assessment that should make it easier for you to approach colleagues, and to begin using these small opportunities to form partnerships.

First, though, I'd like to have you look at this transparency.

STEPS TO FOLLOW

1. Show only the first line of Transparency 88-1. Ask, "Would you rather have the sum on the left or the sum on the right?" Show the second line and ask the same question. Then show the third line and ask the same question. Continue to the last line.

2. Divide the class in half. Ask one half to quietly copy and then add the figures on the left. Have the other half of the class do the same with the figures on the right.

3. Compare the two answers and discuss the fact that things are not always what they seem at first. We are sometimes unshakably convinced that what we are doing is in our (and the organization's) best interests. By learning more about what others are doing, though, we often discover there is a better way to do what we do.

4. Distribute the handout and have them work on it individually for about 10 minutes. Upon completion of the exercise, ask if anyone would like to share his/her thoughts.

DISCUSSION QUESTIONS

✓ Of what small opportunities in the workplace have you taken advantage lately?

✓ Have any of them turned into great enterprises?

238

✓ Thinking beyond your own business, what other business examples can you cite of small opportunities becoming great enterprises?

✓ How can the organization encourage entrepreneurship within its own walls (or "intrapreneurship," as Gifford Pinchot calls it)?

$987654321 $123456789

$87654321 $12345678

$7654321 $1234567

$654321 $123456

$54321 $12345

$4321 $1234

$321 $123

$21 $12

$1 $1

SELF-ASSESSMENT

Directions: After answering the questions as honestly as possible, review them and then outline a partnership plan.

1. Those in the workplace who perform the same processes in which I engage:

_____

2. Those above who probably do the work faster or more accurately than I do:

_____

3. Those in my workplace unit who have special expertise in one aspect of our work:

_____

4. Those with cooperative and/or willing-to-try-anything-once attitudes: _____

_____

5. Those who are inventive, creative, imaginative, good at problem solving: _____

_____

6. Specific aspects of the work in which I consider myself a whiz: _____

_____

7. Critical elements of the work we do: _____

_____

8. Aspects of the work that we could do without (because they are redundant or no longer necessary): _____

_____

9. Aspects of the work about which we hear the most complaints: _____

_____

In view of the preceding information, use the reverse side of this sheet to outline a partnership plan that would allow you and others (partners) to improve an aspect of the work or the work environment. Be as specific as possible.

OVERVIEW: EXTERNAL PARTNERS

In all likelihood, ours is not the only organization in the world that does what we do. Even if we had that unique distinction, we would share some workplace conditions with other organizations. For example, all companies have to provide orientation, pay their employees, and offer training. Most companies have suggestion programs, celebrate the holidays, recognize secretaries during Secretaries Week, or market and advertise the goods and services they offer. All organizations have customers, whose opinions they should be soliciting.

No matter what your organization does, other organizations probably are doing the same thing. The formal overtures being made by your organization to discover how others operate constitute your firm's benchmarking process. External partners are typically eager to share nonproprietary information, because benchmarking presents a win-win opportunity to *gain* knowledge about how to improve certain operations and to *give* knowledge so that others can improve as well.

Learning about the excellent practices in which other organizations engage develops excellence in our own. External benchmarking develops external awareness, broadening our world view. It strips us of the chauvinism that so easily accompanies pride. While self-congratulation and "We're number 1" feelings instill cohesion, they also blind us to the need for growth and continuous improvement.

To create a culture of improvement, our very foundations have to be shaken from time to time. External benchmarking does this—always with the aim of making us better than we are. It pushes us to new levels of achievement as we seek to meet and ultimately exceed the levels attained by world-class competitors.

Benchmarking initiates tend to think of same-industry partners as they undertake the benchmarking process. However, it is possible to improve certain processes by studying other industries. Just-in-time practices have value for *various* manufacturers, as do successful practices that reduce cycle times. Certain beneficial techniques cut across product lines, applying to a number of industries and enhancing many processes.

To continue the excellence acquired from studying the best of the best, organizations need to continuously monitor and correct themselves.

89

UNDECIDABLE AND DECIDABLE FIGURES

OBJECTIVE

To have participants think about what they must do to find **benchmarking partners**

TIME

Approximately 25 minutes

MATERIALS

Transparency 89-1; Handout 89-1: Beginning to Benchmark

MINILECTURE

"Quality is never an accident," John Ruskin asserted, *"it is always the result of intelligent effort."* In their efforts to increase quality, organizations continuously undertake intelligent efforts such as benchmarking. When we benchmark, we essentially compare ourselves to others engaged in similar practices. By so doing, we not only develop a basis for comparison, we can also save time, money, and effort. There is no reason to reinvent wheels when other organizations are more than willing to share their wheel blueprints with those who ask for them.

But if you ask, you must be clear about what you are seeking. Otherwise, you will be wasting your time and the benchmarkee's as well. If you've not carefully defined your needs, you may appear to be asking unanswerable questions for which unclear answers will be given. Unanswerable questions leave receivers wondering what you want. They are like the undecidable figures psychologists present us with. Look at the transparency now and decide—are these rectangular boxes ready to be filled or already-flattened boxes with their sides up? [Show Transparency 89-1.]

STEPS TO FOLLOW

1. After showing the transparency, distribute Handout 89-1. Allow participants 10 to 15 minutes to complete it.

2. Pair off participants and have each person share his/her responses with the partner. Then have the partners do the same.

DISCUSSION QUESTIONS

✓ How and where would you start a benchmarking effort in your firm?

✓ What criteria would you use?

✓ What questions would you ask of your benchmarking partner?

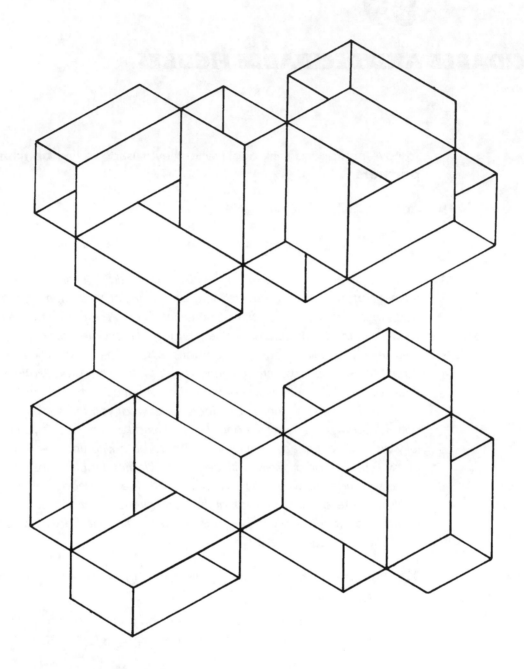

Decide if you can: rectangular boxes or flattened boxes with the sides up?

Reprinted with permission from Harry Turner, *Triad Optical Illusions* (New York: Dover Publications, Inc.).

BEGINNING TO BENCHMARK

Directions: Answer as many questions as you can, as fully as you can. You will discuss your answers with a partner. Take the handout back to work and use it to form and to work with a benchmarking team.

1. Who's the best as far as organizations that do what your organization does?

2. What best practices do you wish to learn more about?

3. What questions will you ask of your benchmarking partner?

4. How can you apply or adapt those practices to avoid mere copying?

5. What decidable figures do you have, can you obtain, to show your benchmarking partner you have a solid understanding of

    Your customer?

    Your processes?

    Your outputs (and their quality)?

    Your systems?

6. What responsibilities will you assign to various members of a benchmarking team?

7. What can you give to your benchmarking partner in return?

8. What will your letter seeking a partner have to say?

9. If you go on a site visit, how much time will it entail and what will you hope to see?

10. What recording instruments will you need to document the data you will be gathering?

90

THINK THE UNTHINKABLE

OBJECTIVE

To stimulate thinking about ideal **benchmarking partners**

TIME

Approximately 20 minutes

MATERIALS

None

MINILECTURE

"At 3M, every division is expected to get 25 percent of its sales each year from products that didn't exist five years earlier." Joe Griffith applauds the spirit of innovation that permeates the strategic thinking of successful companies like 3M. That same kind of thinking permeates the benchmarking of successful companies. It is characterized by a willingness to think the unthinkable—to go, mentally, where none or few have gone before.

To illustrate, a large manufacturing firm, concerned about the length of time it was taking to change over employees on a production line, decided to study the speed with which racing cars were serviced in a pit stop. Another large manufacturing firm, concerned with the length of time it took for orders of their office equipment products to be fulfilled, studied the process employed by a successful mail order company. Subsequently, they were able to reduce the process time by 10 percent.

STEPS TO FOLLOW

1. Have participants work in small groups of three or four. Each shares one process (in which he/she, the work unit, or the organization itself engages) that needs improvement. The other members of the team work with the first speaker to suggest atypical organizations that might be good sources of benchmarking data for improving that process. Encourage them to go beyond the obvious or typical sources.

   The first person takes notes on the ideas (and, it is hoped, takes the ideas back to a benchmarking team). The next person follows the same procedure of describing a process and seeking ideas for how benchmarking data might be obtained.

2. Afterwards, call on one person from each team to share the ideas he/she has garnered.

DISCUSSION QUESTIONS

✓ If yours is a service organization, what things (including processes) do you have in common with other service organizations?

✓ What do you have in common with manufacturing organizations?

✓ What is the name of a service organization that you believe exhibits world-class service?

✓ What is the name of a manufacturing organization that you believe produces world-class products?

✓ What name comes to mind when you think about the best health care facility in the country? The best media organization? The best academic institution?

✓ In view of all the preceding answers, can you find one work practice that you feel needs improvement and one organization from which you could learn to improve?

91

TRIAL AND ERROR RATES

OBJECTIVE   To encourage the production of guidelines for **processes with low error rates**

TIME   Approximately 40 minutes

MATERIALS   None

MINILECTURE   *Richard Buetow observed that, "Best-in-class companies have error rates 500 to 1000 times lower than average." This observation may help to explain why organizations intent on survival are intent on benchmarking. So popular has the trend become that the American Productivity and Quality Center in Houston has established a computerized database of best practices and how to implement them. For organizations that cannot afford consultants or faraway site visits for groups of employees, this information highway may be able to take them to the same destination.*

Assume that you have been asked by the Center to contribute to their International Benchmarking Clearinghouse a best practice and the guidelines that explain how another organization could adopt and implement that practice. We define a best practice here as "a process that has a low rate of errors." Using this definition, what would you cite as a best practice? What guidelines could you share with others about how to replicate the process in their own organization?

STEPS TO FOLLOW
1. Ask participants to work for about 20 minutes to identify a best practice in which they engage and to depict the steps in the process.

2. Ask participants to listen carefully (perhaps even to jot down notes) as you call on each person to state his/her best practice. Advise participants that they will form groups to discuss practices in which they have a shared interest.

3. Have participants form their own groups based on common best practices. Within these groups, have them share ideas and guidelines.

DISCUSSION QUESTIONS
✓ Is the best practice you identified the same one your boss would have identified? Why or why not?

✓ Is it the same one your primary customer would have identified? Why or why not?

✓ Why do you feel this particular process has such a low error rate?

✓ Do others who engage in the same process in your organization have an equally low error rate? Explain why or why not.

✓ Cite the advantages and disadvantages of visiting a benchmarking partner to see their operations.

OVERVIEW: THE BENCHMARKING STRATEGY

You will find other TQM-committed organizations surprisingly willing to share information about what they do and how they do it. However, they are typically unwilling to waste time. Before you approach a similar-industry organization or a department or individual within it, make certain you follow these steps:

✓ Learn what your organization is already doing in terms of benchmarking. Find out if someone has already been appointed to conduct a benchmarking program. If so, ask if you could work with that person. If not, obtain permission from your manager to contact other companies.

✓ Have ready and show your manager the letter you will send to the appropriate individual in another company. The letter should specify what information you are seeking, how it will be used, and what you can offer the other organization in return.

✓ Once you have received the information, write a formal letter of appreciation. In it, ask if you may contact the person to discuss the information further (or possibly even to arrange a site visit).

✓ Keep your boss apprised not only of what you are receiving but also of what you are sending.

✓ Synthesize the new knowledge you have acquired and share it with others—in a formal report to your boss and/or in an informal report to your team. Let your benchmarking efforts be the catalyst for subsequent action to improve your operations.

✓ Attempt to establish an ongoing communication exchange with your benchmarking partner so that you can make each other aware of new developments.

✓ Consider forming a consortium with several benchmarking partners. The partners can meet periodically to trade ideas and can even arrange an annual conference to include others in this mutually beneficial exchange of ideas. This exchange could also be handled by an electronic "bulletin board."

92

NUMBERS AND NUMBERS OF STEPS

OBJECTIVE   To encourage formulation of a **benchmarking process**

TIME   Approximately 20 minutes

MATERIALS   Flip chart and marking pen

MINILECTURE   *"Benchmarking is not for the half-hearted."* Jeremy Main refers to the whole-hearted attempt that individuals must make if they wish to become full partners in the benchmarking process. In prebenchmarking days, companies would buy and take apart a competitor's product, hoping to learn the secrets behind the competitor's industrial success. This "reverse engineering" has been replaced by the popular, legal, and ethical practice of benchmarking. The replacement is evident in the substitution for the word steal in the everyday expression, "Beg, borrow, or benchmark." Businesses today are willing to share information about best-in-class processes. Such sharing can lead to win-win situations.

Industrial espionage, it seems, is going the way of international espionage. Less than ethical ploys to acquire information are no longer necessary in this era of quality cooperation. Before we examine ways to ethically acquire information, let's have some fun with an underhanded trick. Do I have a volunteer?

STEPS TO FOLLOW   **1.** Station the volunteer near the flip chart which is positioned so that the class can see read it but you cannot. Ask the volunteer to write his/her age on the flip chart and then add 90 to the age. The volunteer then crosses off the first digit on the left of that total, *adds* that first digit to the remaining two digits, and then tells you the total.

2. When you hear that result, silently add 9 and you can tell the person his/her age.

3. Point out that such sly tactics are fun for games but unnecessary among benchmarking partners.

4. Ask participants if they are familiar with any well-established processes, such as the four-phase system of IBM, the nine-step approach of AT&T, or the ten-step method of Xerox. Samuel Bookhart, head of benchmarking for DuPont, tells benchmarkers, "Don't get hung up on the numbers-of-steps game. But you do need a process." The process boils down to finding relevant best practices and figuring out how to make them work in the organization.

5. Have participants assume that, in return for benchmarking data, another company has asked for examples of best-in-class practices from their company. Ask participants to make a list of all the processes in which they engage during a typical week. Then have them place stars next to the one or two that they feel are operating at peak proficiency.

6. In groups of two or three, they should briefly tell *why* the process(es) operates as well as it does.

✓ One possible danger of benchmarking is that teams might, as a result of benchmarking information, make changes that could negatively impact other departments. What could a benchmarking team do to avoid this problem?

✓ L. L. Bean receives so many requests to become benchmarking partners that they have had to limit sharing information to companies with a genuine interest in quality. How would your own organization demonstrate that they indeed have a genuine interest?

✓ Discuss possible legal/ethical issues that benchmarking partners might need to address.

93

BENCHMARKING KEYS

OBJECTIVE

To promote thinking about **key processes** as a prelude to determining which processes to **benchmark**

TIME

Approximately 25 minutes, if there are at least two people from every organization represented in the class
About 15 minutes, if participants represent totally different companies

MATERIALS

Flip chart; marking pen; Handout 93-1: Key Practices

MINILECTURE

"Too many companies suffer from their refusal to believe others can do things better." Robert C. Camp explains what keeps some organizations from launching a benchmarking effort. While every company should be justifiably proud of certain processes and their results, not every process is being executed as efficiently as it might be.

    The hard part about benchmarking is first determining which processes are the most critical. Having isolated the key processes, the next step is to decide which are most in need of improvement. This narrowed list should then be juxtaposed with customer expectations and finally with best-in-class practices.

    Benchmarking partners, though, did not achieve their levels of excellence by wasting time. To approach them without having done your homework is to waste their time. I have a handout that assists you in refining your thinking about which practices to pursue. The trick is to subject all processes to the same scrutiny—even those you favor or believe to be superior.

    Let me first show you another trick to illustrate how favored practices produce more of the same. When we continue with successful processes, they yield what they've always yielded. Benchmarking could mean they yield more.

STEPS TO FOLLOW

1. Ask a volunteer to select a favorite number between 1 and 9. Then proceed to write on the flip chart. "1 2 3 4 5 6 7 9." (The 8 is purposely omitted.)

2. No matter what number the volunteer chose, mentally multiply the number (after he/she tells you what it is) by 9 to obtain the *product* we need. Then tell the volunteer to multiply the 1-2-3-4-5-6-7-9 sequence by the product. The result is a string of his/her favorite number. For example, if 7 is the favorite number:

```
    1 2 3 4 5 6 7 9
        ∞         6 3    (the product of 7 ∞ 9)
   ─────────────────
    3 7 0 3 7 0 3 7
  7 4 0 7 4 0 7 4
  ─────────────────
  7 7 7 7 7 7 7 7 7
```

3. Briefly mention that it is natural to permit successful or "favored" processes to escape scrutiny, but *every* process can be improved. Distribute Handout 93-1 and have them work on it individually.

4. After approximately 15 minutes, have each person join another person from his/her organization and compare their responses.

✓ The danger in having faith in one's own excellence is that it occassionally prevents us from discovering other practices that may be "more excellent" than our own. What are some practices in your own work, your own work unit, or your own company that have not been examined for a long time because the results have been satisfactory?

✓ Think about your most successful "competitors." Do you think they would identify the same key practices you have identified? Explain.

✓ Which practices add the most value for customers?

HANDOUT 93-1

KEY PRACTICES

1. Think about your department or work unit. What are the processes for which they are responsible? What are all the things your department *does*? List them here.

	Why key?	Why key for customer?
1.		
2.		
3.		
4.		
5.		
6.		
7.		
8.		
9.		
10.		
11.		
12.		
13.		
14.		
15.		
16.		
17.		
18.		
19		
20.		

2. Go back and put stars next to the key processes.

3. In the first column, explain why the starred processes are key.

4. Draw a triangle beside the processes that *customers* would identify as key. In the second column, explain why you selected certain processes as key for customer.

5. Acknowledging that resources are limited and that it is difficult for team members to find time to do team work, which one of the processes you originally listed would you recommend for a benchmarking team to study? _____

255

SECTION 12

REENGINEERING, REINVENTING, REDEFINING

A natural outgrowth of the Quality movement are three "buzzwords" that capture the thrust behind continuous improvement: in a manufacturing environment, we may have to **reengineer** our processes in order to consistently increase the quality of the product we provide and the speed by which we provide it. The identification and elimination of nonvalue-added steps may even lead to a reduction in the cost of the product.

In a service industry, such as government, we may have to **reinvent** the structures that were established in different times, for different reasons.

In our own organizations, we may have to **redefine** the work, the workers, the work units, and the work environment.

These buzzwords and their connotations of excellence will be examined in this section.

OVERVIEW: PARALLELS WITH THE QUALITY MOVEMENT

The Quality movement asks us to identify and eliminate waste. Whether we are reengineering, reinventing, or redefining, we do so to streamline work processes, to ensure that each step adds value and to confirm that the customer is willing to pay for what we are doing.

Some in the Quality movement believe in a gradual, incremental approach to change (sometimes referred to as the *kaizen* approach). Others advocate a complete and radical transformation. Whichever course is chosen, the efforts affect every department—from engineering to finance, from manufacturing to marketing. The desire to reengineer precedes the ability. In time, every employee will be able to look at a process and ask the essential question, "If I were to design this for the first time, what steps would I include?"

How much an organization is willing to start from scratch in its self-examination and subsequent makeover is how much it is willing to reengineer and reinvent. (Redefining can be done at any stage and to any extent.)

This new breath of inventive air is infiltrating corporate board rooms and shop floors alike. Reengineers are moving beyond basing business practices on a familiar body of ideas, beyond creating new products from traditional stock. More proactive than reactive, more rebellious than rote, they are daring to alter traditional processes or perhaps to discard them altogether.

It has been said that, on the most basic level, "it all coheres." Looking at the principles that drive the Quality movement, one finds cohesion with the principles of reengineering and reinvention. All are concerned, at the most fundamental level, with improving how business is conducted.

Standard operating procedures have to become unstandardized. They need to be reexamined, reanalyzed, and recalculated in terms of what provides the greatest value for customers. All of this has to be done before we can decide which procedures should indeed become standard once more.

94

ALL WORK IS PROCESS

OBJECTIVE

To develop awareness of the need to **analyze and document carefully the processes to be reengineered**

TIME

5 to 30 minutes, depending on the ability of the working team

MATERIALS

Transparency 94-1: Disk Stack Rules; Handout 94-1: Observer's Form; washable ink pen or washable marker; two sheets of paper for each team

MINILECTURE

Alfred North Whitehead was far ahead of his time when he noted that "the process itself is the actuality." Whether we are speaking of the Quality movement or the reengineering/reinvention movement, we are looking at how things are done so that we can figure out how to do them better. The actuality is always the process—what transforms an input to an output.

Sometimes process action teams—as they work to identify, understand, measure, and improve processes—learn that the process is more complex than they had realized or that the process is better designed than they had anticipated. Sometimes they opt to reengineer the whole process or to salvage parts of it.

I'll need teams of eight to analyze and document a process that represents one of the oldest puzzles in the world. It derives from the legend surrounding the Tower of Brahma, which was constructed of 64 disks, stacked one on top of the other. If monks, the legend goes, were to transfer the disks—according to these rules [show Transparency 94-1 and leave it up throughout the exercise]— and if they were working at the rate of one disk transferred in one second, they would need trillions of years to complete the restacking of the tower!

Fortunately, today, you will be working with a tower that has only seven disks. So you will need to make only 127 moves. And these "disks" are human hands so it will be a little more interesting. (By the way, it is possible to complete this task in a mere 5 minutes, although most of my classes need much more time.) Here is your assignment:

1. *There will be seven people in a team. Each person will write one number from 1 to 7 on his or her hand. (The eighth person will be your Observer/Documenter.)*

2. *Notice I am laying two sheets of paper here. Each team will stack their hands in order on the left-hand sheet, with 7 on the bottom and 1 on the top.*

3. *The winner of the game will be the team that first transfers the hands to another sheet of paper, ending with them stacked in the same order we began with: 7 on the bottom and 1 on top. Make certain your successful sequence is documented, in case it has to be repeated.*

STEPS TO FOLLOW

1. Divide the class into teams of eight. (Each team needs one Observer/Documenter.) If there are "extra" particfipants, they can serve as general observers.

2. Quickly repeat the instructions in the minilecture and ask if there are any questions. Then proceed, noting how long it took the teams to complete the assignment.

DISCUSSION QUESTIONS

✓ How did it affect you to know that it was possible to solve the puzzle in only five minutes?

✓ What is your general response to challenging problems?

✓ How can an organization increase receptivity to difficult but doable tasks?

✓ Did leadership emerge in your team?

✓ Did anyone attempt to alleviate the stress and/or confusion that is typically part of such an assignment?

✓ If your organization is reengineering processes, has it carefully documented the steps involved in *existing* processes? Are there flow diagrams depicting both the existing and the ideal versions?

DISK STACK RULES

1. You can move only one hand at a time.

2. You can move only the hand on top of the stack.

3. Never place a higher-number hand on top of a lower-number hand.

OBSERVER'S FORM

1. Was everyone clear about the task?

_____

_____

_____

_____

_____

2. How well did they handle time?

_____

_____

_____

_____

_____

3. Were they successful? Why or why not?

_____

_____

_____

_____

_____

4. Tell the extent/frequency with which you were asked by the team to document the process.

_____

_____

_____

_____

5. Whether or not you were asked, record the successful sequence needed to restack the hands in the same order as that of the original stack.

_____

_____

_____

_____

_____

95

FROM REAL TO IDEAL TO REAL AGAIN

OBJECTIVE

To foster comparisons between **what is** and **what is possible**

TIME

Approximately 15 minutes

MATERIALS

Transparency 95-1: WIN/WIP Model

MINILECTURE

Jonathan Swift defined vision as "the art of seeing things impossible." Reengineers and Total Quality managers alike are, in a sense, seeing things that are now impossible to see, things that they believe will take shape in time and be visible to others in the organization.

A simple technique that enables you to see what is impossible to see is the WIN/WIP cube.

STEPS TO FOLLOW

1. Show Transparency 95-1. Ask participants to reproduce it on their own papers and then to fill in the quadrants based on the four prompts.

2. Have participants work in dyads or triads—from the same work units if possible—to share their responses.

DISCUSSION QUESTIONS

✓ What vision does your organization have for its own future?

✓ What vision do the members of your work unit have for the way the work unit will function five years from today?

✓ What things were not possible to see five years ago that are visible in the workplace today?

✓ What will it take for your work unit to move from "what is" to "what is possible"?

✓ What new learning will your work unit have to acquire to make the transition?

GAME STRETCHER

(10 minutes) What other prompts could you place on such a square to yield insights about processes that could benefit from reengineering efforts?

WIN/WIP MODEL FOR PROCESSES TO BE REENGINEERED

	What is	**What is possible**
Now		
In 5 years		

96

INSIDE/OUTSIDE CHANGES

OBJECTIVE   To stimulate interest in **reengineering** as a means of **improving quality**

TIME   Approximately 15 minutes

MATERIALS   Transparency 96-1; Handout 96-1: Less Better/More Worse

MINILECTURE   *Take a look now at Tom Peters' assertion* [show transparency]. *To do better, organizations need to take serious looks at the way they do business. They need to decide which processes should be subjected to the questions associated with reengineering scrutiny:*

✓ *Is this process necessary?*

✓ *If we were to design it for the first time, how would it look?*

✓ *If we had to cut the time (or cost or steps) by 50 percent, what would we eliminate?*

Questions such as these lie at the heart of continuous improvement.

STEPS TO FOLLOW   **1.** Assemble groups of five or six. Distribute Handout 96-1.

2. Ask for volunteers to share some of the insights gleaned from consideration of the Peters' quotation.

DISCUSSION QUESTIONS   ✓ Take any one of your work processes. Answer the following questions about it:

Is this process necessary?

How much value does it add?

If we were to design it for the first time, how would it look?

If we had to streamline it by cutting the time (or cost or steps or staff) by 50 percent, what would we eliminate?

✓ How can organizations encourage questions like these to be asked periodically at staff meetings?

✓ How does reengineering a process differ from improving a process?

GAME STRETCHER   (10 minutes) Have groups discuss what Peters meant when he declared that, "Good quality is a stupid idea." [*Note:* The full context of his statement refers to the fact that good quality in and of itself is not sufficient for survival or success.]

"If we're not getting more, better, faster than *they* are getting more, better, faster, then we're getting less better or more worse."

—Tom Peters

LESS BETTER/MORE WORSE

Directions: Think about your organization. If you were to get more, in the most positive sense of the word, what would *more* mean?

_____

_____

_____

What exactly does *better* mean in terms of your organization?

_____

_____

_____

What exactly does *faster* mean in terms of your firm's operations?

_____

_____

_____

What would *less better* mean in your organization?

_____

_____

_____

What would *more worse* mean in your organization?

_____

_____

_____

What outside forces oare propelling your organization to do *more, better, faster*?

_____

_____

_____

What forces inside the organization are pushing for that as well?

_____

_____

_____

97

CONTEXTUAL CLUES

OBJECTIVE	To encourage reduction in **learning curve cycle time**
TIME	Approximately 20 minutes
MATERIALS	Transparency 97-1
MINILECTURE	*"You think you understand the situation, but what you don't understand is that the situation just changed."* This popular advertisement from Putnam Investments says it all. We no longer have the luxury of time on the learning curve. Living in the Nanosecond Nineties, we must absorb information—lots of information—quickly and then apply it to our work. Continuous learning and continuous improvement are required of today's employees.* *To illustrate, I am going to give you a problem to solve. We will note how long it takes for us as a group to solve it. I will then show you two other, similar problems. Again, we will note the length of time it takes for us to find a solution. In all likelihood, we will be able to shorten our learning curve cycle time because we will have figured out what is required to solve the problem after the first attempt. Work as quickly as you can.*
STEPS TO FOLLOW	**1.** Show Transparency 97-1, making certain to show just the first problem. [*Note:* A sheet of paper can be used to cover up the other problems until the group is ready to tackle them.] Make note of how long it takes for the first *correct* answer to be offered. The answer here is none because unlisted numbers will not appear in the book. **2.** Before showing the next problem, emphasize what we have learned: that we need to attend to the context of the problem. Slowing down to understand the problem is often faster than rushing to solve it without clearly understanding it. The solution, then, is impossible unless we truly attend to each word. We need to know what the problem is asking of us before we can solve the problem. Show the second problem. Note how long it takes this time. (Remember to cover up the third problem.) The correct answer is "43" because we were to divide it by one-half not divide it *in* half. **3.** Do the same thing with the final problem, the answer for which is the same number: 987,654,321. Halving it and then doubling it yields the original.
DISCUSSION QUESTIONS	✓ How carefully does your team attend to problem definition before beginning problem solution?

✓ What specific things could a team leader do to ensure complete understanding?

✓ Could a problem in one area become more of a problem (or less of a problem) if it were placed in a different context? Explain.

✓ For what work-related activities have you shortened your learning curve cycle time?

Seventeen percent of the people in a town have unlisted phone numbers. If you choose 450 names at random from the phone book, what is the expected number who will have unlisted numbers?

Divide 20 by ½ and add 3. What is the total?

How much is twice one half of 987,654,321?

OVERVIEW: ANALYSIS OF MACRO- AND MICROPRACTICES

When an organization examines itself from a macroperspective, it considers the larger issues and asks related tough questions:

For what purpose does our organization exist?

Why do we do what we do?

Are we doing the right thing?

Who are our customers?

What do our customers really want?

When an individual or small work unit undertakes a similar examination, it operates from a microperspective—a consideration of the important issues that influence a smaller sphere of influence. The individual might ask:

How can I improve my work processes?

Who receives the output of the work I do?

How aware am I of what the receiving person expects of the output?

How aware is the receiver of why the output exists as it does?

This introspection is a prelude to the actual redesign of work processes. It lays the groundwork and assures that the need for improvement is valid. It helps in preparing the problem statement and in establishing targets.

The problem—whether considered from the macro- or the microscale—next undergoes analysis to ascertain root causes. Possible countermeasures are considered, and one or several are selected for implementation. If in fact the root cause of the problem is corrected with the countermeasure (if the data offer proof of improvement), the individual or the team works to prevent the problem from occurring again in the future.

The primary difference between process improvement in the Quality mode and process improvement in the reengineering mode is that the latter mode says, essentially, "Even if it ain't broke, maybe we should break it."

98

TRANSFORMATIONS

OBJECTIVE　　　　　To emphasize that the **organizational culture** must be examined and made ready for **reinvention**

TIME　　　　　　　Approximately 15 minutes

MATERIALS　　　　Transparency 98-1: Transforming the Culture; flip chart paper (ideally four flip charts); marking pens

MINILECTURE　　　*"The reinvention of the corporation entails cultural transformation."* Shoshana Zuboff's insight reminds us that nothing happens unless the people want it to happen. Strong leaders in an organization are able to persuade people at all levels that the changes being proposed are not only in the best interest of the organization itself but also in the best interest of individual constituents.

Reinvention, as she asserts, means transforming the way we think—about ourselves, about the organization, about the work, about the customer. Mind-sets have to widen so that new ideas can be embraced. Paradigms have to shift so that new possibilities can be explored. Partner relationships have to form to keep organizations fit enough to survive.

STEPS TO FOLLOW　　**1.** Divide the class into four large teams.

2. Each team is to add as many rhyming pairs as possible to the list of words depicting the changes that may need to occur if reinvention is to succeed.

3. Post the chart paper lists and ask for a volunteer to compile a master list and to share it with the editor of the organization's newsletter.

DISCUSSION QUESTIONS　　✓ What indications have you found of your organization's interest in reinventing itself and/or reengineering its processes?

✓ How would you describe your existing culture?

✓ If your title were the Minister of Corporate Culture, what would you do to make the culture more receptive to reinvention?

272

TRANSFORMING THE CULTURE

<u>FROM</u>

me

status quo

<u>TO</u>

we

status: go

99

REINVENTING THE SOFT SIDE OF QUALITY

OBJECTIVE

To illustrate that some aspects of organizational success are difficult to quantify and therefore difficult to **reinvent**

TIME

Approximately 30 minutes

MATERIALS

Handout 99-1: The Human Side of Quality

MINILECTURE

"Who keeps company with a wolf," Henry Cannon points out, "will learn to howl." In the world of benchmarking, those howls might be interpreted as successful actions. Those who study such actions can learn to imitate or apply them to their own less than successful practices. Reinvention teams are then formed on the basis of what is learned from benchmarking data that have been gathered.

But not all aspects of "wolfness" are as easy to observe as the howls. Similarly, benchmarkers sometimes find it difficult to understand exactly what makes successful companies truly successful. For example, a McKinsey study found that world-class companies are able to generate new products two and one-half times faster than the industry average, at one-half the cost.

A benchmarking partner, eager to learn how this is done, could study the whole manufacturing process from birth of the concept to shipment of the product, and could still fail to understand the nonquantifiable, intangible aspects of quality—its soft side, if you will—that make such speed and profit possible. A site visit may reveal information about the manufacturing process but nothing at all about attitudes, the management style, the communications flow, the morale, the history, the relationships, etc.

The handout I'd like you to work on now asks that you think about the harder-to-define aspects of quality organizations and then to think about which of them should be reinvented in your own organization.

STEPS TO FOLLOW

1. Distribute Handout 99-1 and allow about 10 minutes for its completion.

2. Have participants work in teams of six to share their responses. Then ask them to outline an article that might be written for the company newsletter or a white paper to be circulated to various departments or yet-to-be-formed reinvention teams. The main thrust of the article is how to obtain data on the human aspects of manufacturing or service success.

DISCUSSION QUESTIONS

✓ Assume for a moment that the skills and fees of all physicians were the same. What soft side factors would help you decide on one physician over the others?

✓ How could those factors be quantified?

✓ Think of an excellent organization about which you have first- or second-hand information. What constitutes the excellence that you associate with that company? Which aspects of the excellence could be studied?

GAME STRETCHER If someone in the class enjoys writing, have that person take the outline and convert it to an actual article.

THE HUMAN SIDE OF QUALITY

Directions: For each of the following criteria, rate your own organization on a scale of Poor, Good, or Best. Then tell which facts led you to the rating. Finally, explain what measures could be used to gather data on the factors that constitute the soft side or the human side of quality.

Factor	Rating	Facts	Measurement
1. Morale	_____		
2. Pride	_____		
3. Attitudes	_____		
4. Co-worker relationships	_____		
5. Supervisor/ subordinate relationships	_____		
6. Management style	_____		
7. Joy in the workplace	_____		
8. Communications	_____		
9. Stress levels	_____		

100

FOLLOW YOUR BLISS

OBJECTIVE To encourage thinking about **reinvention possibilities**

TIME Approximately 15 minutes

MATERIALS None

MINILECTURE *"Reinvention means, from time to time, following your bliss." The words of Tom Peters give us pause. They can be likened perhaps to Alfred North Whitehead's comment that "romance precedes precision." It is easier to reinvent the part of our work that fascinates us than to rethink the steps of a process we do not find especially interesting. While the organization's leaders must analyze every major process or function of the organization, individuals must also scrutinize their work. We begin, of course, with critical processes. But, as Peters suggests, we can also occasionally pursue avenues of interest. Usually, they produce important payoffs related to profitability or productivity.*

I'm going to ask you now to identify the one part of your job that you most enjoy. In terms of actual work processes, what do you most like to do?

STEPS TO FOLLOW

1. Form small teams of three or four people. Each person shares with the others one part of his/her work that is especially intriguing. One speaker then begins to explore—with input and questions from the others—how that work element could be reinvented. How would the speaker, in other words, design the work or work element if he/she had full authority to reinvent it? Encourage each speaker to take notes on the discussion. Ideally, these notes could be taken back to the workplace and shared with a reinvention team.

2. The other members of the group share their thoughts in the same way.

DISCUSSION QUESTIONS

✓ It is easy to pursue "blissful" work interests. But how can the organization develop a willingness to pursue the less than blissful aspects of work and the work environment?

✓ Have you discovered, of your own volition, shortcuts to the work you do? If so, how did those discoveries come about? Have you shared them with others?

✓ Are improvement teams in your organization assembled by management? Are they ever composed of people interested in a particular process? What data drive the decisions regarding which projects the teams will undertake?

✓ In your opinion, how should reinvention teams be formed?

101

4-IMP PLAN

OBJECTIVE   To encourage involvement in **reinvention efforts**

TIME   Approximately 15 minutes

MATERIALS   Transparency 101-1

MINILECTURE   *"Commitment," asserts Ed McElroy, "gives us new power." Empowered employees continue the cycle by becoming more committed and more empowered. Developing commitment, though, is no easy task. Organizational leaders—official and unofficial ones—will find that there should be a plan for increasing commitment to reinvention. To talk about it is not enough. One must be talking to the right people, about the right things, for the right purpose.*

The 4-Imp Plan will help you think about involving others in your work unit in the important work of reinvention.

STEPS TO FOLLOW   **1.** Form teams of five or six. They are to assume they are reinventing the suggestion process in an organization. Show Transparency 101-1. Ask the teams to supply ideas based on these four words:

Impact   (Who would be affected by a typical reinvention team's redesign of a work process)?

Importance   (What is important to those individuals? What are their concerns?)

Impediments   (What organizational barriers stand between the reinvention team and their ultimate success?)

Impel   (What specific actions would a team take to urge others to participate in the reinvention efforts?)

2. Ask each team to work with another team to share their ideas.

DISCUSSION QUESTIONS   ✓ How is your work unit involved with new directions that are set in your organization?

✓ What factors increase your own commitment to an effort?

4-IMP PLAN

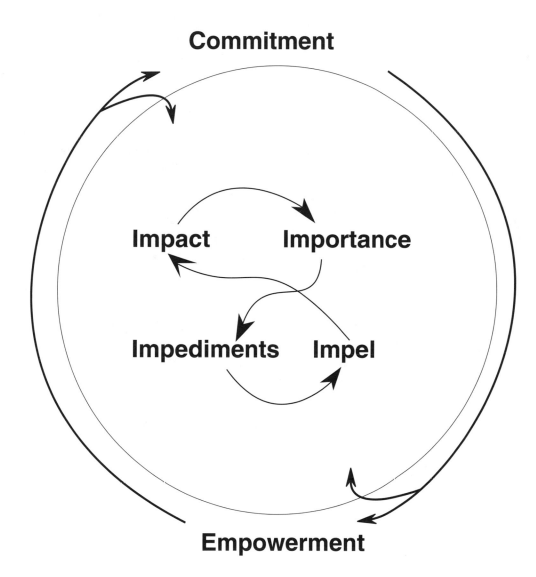

Commitment

Impact   Importance

Impediments   Impel

Empowerment

APPENDIX:
QUOTATIONS AND THEIR USE

All the world loves a quote. And the collection of quotations on the following pages can be used in a number of ways.

1. Make copies of them and distribute them as token gifts to the "winners" of competitive games.

2. Distribute the collection to class participants, and ask them the following questions in relation to the quotations:

>Which comes closest to your boss's philosophy?
>
>Which comes closest to your own?
>
>Which represents the way you wish your organization could function?
>
>Which is most valuable for teams?
>
>Which would serve best to inspire employees?
>
>If you were the CEO of your organization, which would you select as a motto for daily corporate living?
>
>Which would encourage continuous learning?

3. Have participants paraphrase one of the sayings to make it relevant to their own organizations. For example, number 18, from John Naisbitt, reads, "We are drowning in information but starved for knowledge." A paraphrase might be, "We are drowning in regulations, but thirsting for a policy."

4. Use the quotes as a means of practicing stratification. Ask small groups to stratify the quotes into five or six categories. Sample stratifications, for example, could be:

>Problem solving/decision making
>
>Organizational practices
>
>Psychological considerations
>
>Learning
>
>Challenges
>
>Interpersonal relationships

5. To boost creativity, have participants create their own pithy, meaningful quotations. They might strive for humor, external awareness, motivation, or any other appropriate tone or theme.

6. Use the list as a stimulus for recalling other favorite or applicable quotations. The recollected list can also be stratified. Or it can be used to help teams develop their skills with consensus as they work to select a favorite quotation.

7. As an exercise in communication, have participants examine the language of the quotations to determine the elements that help create memorable quotations. Compile a list of these and encourage their use.

QUOTATIONS

1. "We are what we repeatedly do. Excellence, then, is not an act but a habit." —Aristotle

2. "Quality will be accomplished project by project and in no other way." —Dr. Joseph M. Juran

3. "Drive out fear." —Dr. W. Edwards Deming

4. "If there are going to be any visceral decisions around here, I'd like to use my own viscera." —Thomas J. Watson, Jr.

5. "Assume the best and that is usually what happens." —Philip B. Crosby

6. "The greatest losses are unknown and unknowable." —Dr. W. Edwards Deming

7. "Eliminate turf wars." —Dr. Joseph M. Juran

8. "The quickest way to turn around is for the management of companies to take charge of the education of the people and help them to learn the necessary things." —Philip B. Crosby

9. "The path to greatness is always along with others." —Baltaser Gracian

10. "Big people monopolize the listening. Small people monopolize the talking." —David Schwartz

11. "The very difficulty of a problem evokes abilities or talents which otherwise, in happy times, never emerge to shine." —Horace

12. "I swear I can see beauty in a hamburger bun." —Ray Kroc

13. "What is the point of doing something very efficiently that should not be done at all?" —Peter Drucker

14. "When you're through changing, you're through." —Bruce Barton

15. "Innovation has never come through bureaucracy and hierarchy. It's always come from individuals." —John Scully

16. "The measure of success is not whether you have a tough problem to deal with, but whether it's the same problem you had last year." —John Foster Dulles

17. "You seldom accomplish very much by yourself. You must get the assistance of others." —Henry J. Kaiser

18. "We are drowning in information but starved for knowledge." —John Naisbitt

19. "You can sometimes fool the fans, but you can never fool the players." —Jack Stack

20. "There's no mystery to satisfying your customer. Build them a product and treat them with respect. It's that simple." —Lee Iacocca

21. "The customer is our employer." —Joe L. Griffith

22. "To become a great bullfighter, one must learn how the bull thinks." —Spanish proverb

23. "The task of the leader is to get his people from where they are to where they have never been." —Henry Kissinger

24. "Anything you do is everything you do." —Buddhist saying

25. "When working toward the solution of a problem, it always helps if you know the answer." —John Peer

About the Author

Marlene Caroselli, Ed.D., is a professional trainer specializing in the area of quality and continuous improvement. Her previous books include the best-selling *Quality-Driven Designs: 36 Activities to Reinforce TQM Concepts* and several others for trainers and managers. Dr. Caroselli holds a Doctorate in Education degree from the University of Rochester, Graduate School of Education and Human Development. She is based in Rochester, New York, where she is Director of the Center for Professional Development.